THE FOREST OF DEAN
IN WARTIME

HUMPHREY PHELPS

ALAN SUTTON PUBLISHING LIMITED

First published in the United Kingdom in 1995
Alan Sutton Publishing Ltd · Phoenix Mill · Far Thrupp · Stroud
Gloucestershire

British Library Cataloguing in Publication Data

A catalogue record for this book is available from the British Library

ISBN 0-7509-1179-4

For my Granddaughter, Carlaina,
these glimpses of wartime life
in the Forest.

Typeset in 12/13 Bembo Mono.
Typesetting and origination by
Alan Sutton Publishing Limited.
Printed in Great Britain by
Ebenezer Baylis, Worcester.

CONTENTS

Pte M.W. Burns, Glos Regt, with his wife and son, by White House in Mitcheldean, October 1939. Pte Burns was killed in France on 19 May 1940, the first service man from Mitcheldean to be killed in the war. He left home immediately after this photograph was taken; his family never saw him again.

CHAPTER ONE

AS IT WAS

It was the time of the blackout, of regulations and restrictions. It was a time of rationing and rumours. It was wartime.

Even before the war began, many families in the Forest of Dean had experienced rationing. Coal mining was the principal industry but the collieries were not working every shift – 'We didn't know from day to day if there'd be work, we had to listen for the hooters'. In those days boys of fourteen were working in the pit; crawling on hands and knees, dragging hods of coal behind them. Jobs were hard to find and in the Forest there was virtually no employment for girls.

After the war began the collieries were working every shift. Instead of not being allowed to go to work, the miners were not allowed to be absent from work. Other men and women found employment in the factories engaged on war work – the majority travelled by special buses to the aircraft factories at Brockworth. 'The long hours of work, the greyness of everything, the old bus just able to get up the hill, full of exhausted grey-faced factory workers, doing twelve hour shifts, day in, day out. When the bus returned at night its occupants fell out clutching their belongings which included gas masks. . . .'

But before that, the evacuees came, clutching their gas masks and few belongings – strange children coming to a strange world. Most of them had never heard of the Forest of Dean. And the Forest was a world unto itself in those days, and its people spoke a language scarcely comprehensible to a stranger. No bombs fell in the evacuees' home towns during the first months of the war and most of them went back home.

Soldiers also came. They felled the oaks, chestnuts, beeches. . . . The Military commandeered halls, houses, pubs and erected

Nissen huts to accommodate the soldiers; the Canadians at Broadwell were under canvas. Much later in the war, the US troops came – white soldiers and black soldiers, who were kept in rigidly segregated units. The colour bar was something new to the Foresters and they did not like it.

The American Invasion had a great impact on the Forest. Suddenly it seemed that they were everywhere. They rode about the Forest in jeeps, with one leg thrust nonchalantly over the side. 'In all my life,' remarked my aged grandfather, 'I've never seen anything like it.'

Initials proliferated:

AFS	Auxiliary Fire Service
ARP	Air Raid Precautions
LDV	Local Defence Volunteers
SP	Special Policeman
WLA	Women's Land Army
WTC	Women's Timber Corps
WVS	Women's Voluntary Service

In the summer of 1940, with the threat of imminent invasion, men hurried to join the LDV. They had no weapons, their defences were puny. What chance had they against the trained invaders with modern weapons that were expected any day? But this did not deter them. It was, when all is said, a great time in British history.

Long after the danger of invasion had passed, men were compelled to attend Home Guard parades two or three times a week. It must have been irksome to those who did a full and strenuous job, and probably had a garden to cultivate as well. Churchill ordered the issue of pikes to the Home Guard twelve months after it had been formed. This angered the Home Guard and made it the object of ridicule. If any of those pikes ever reached the Forest, someone had the sense to keep them secret.

Everybody was expected to do something, and most people were compelled to do so, in addition to their regular work. Some of it was useful, some of it just gratified those with a desire to order people about. With so many local groups and volunteer services it was, as noted by a Forester who did serve in the army, 'a wonder how they found anybody for the Forces'.

It was a time of make do and mend. Potato Pete made his debut, Lord Woolton introduced his Pie and whale steak appeared. Stockings were difficult to obtain. Some girls painted their legs with liquid make-up and drew seams with an eyebrow pencil. Blanch of Coleford advertised 'Blanch's Liquid Stockings. A real winner. It imparts to the legs an appearance of sheer silk stockings – does not stain – is easily removed and delicately perfumed.' Coupons or permits were needed for most essential goods unless, of course, you were 'in the know', or had something to trade illegally – bacon, pork, lamb, eggs, or some other commodity in short supply.

Photographic films were scarce or unobtainable, although in August 1940 Clifford Hughes of Lydney was advertising 'all size films'. If people had wandered round many of the places in the Forest with a camera, they would soon have found themselves in trouble.

Despite these hardships, the Foresters were generous when it came to the war effort. The Forest of Dean, in conjunction with Monmouth and Chepstow, had a Spitfire Fund and raised £7,675 17s. 3d. which was sent to the Minister of Aircraft Production.

The Monmouth, Chepstow and Forest of Dean Spitfire Fund raised over £7,000.

The coldest winter for years occurred in 1940; in January there were snowfalls and the Severn at Minsterworth was frozen over. It was very cold from January to May 1941, and 1942 was also very cold with a lot of snow in January. It was mild and wet in 1943 but snow fell again in 1944. There were heavy snowfalls in January 1945 and in some places in the Forest children could not get to school for a week or more. In that year there were twenty-two wet days in June.

The war brought men, women and children to the Forest. It also took Foresters away from the Forest, some never to return. By January 1940 more than 500 Forest men were already in the

An advertisement from December 1939 for duty free cigarettes and tobacco.

Armed Forces. A 'Forest Smokes Fund' was started to provide them with cigarettes. Large cigarettes then cost 11s. 8d. for 200, smaller cigarettescost 6s. for 120. Cigarettes for Forces men serving overseas were duty free and considerably cheaper.

Watts of Lydney were advertising bicycles from £4 19s. 9d., the Pillowell and Yorkley Co-op was advertising 'Gents Suits', made to measure for £2 6s. 6d.

School meals started in the Forest. Ruardean Hill School was the first to provide meals, which cost 4d., and other Forest Schools followed this example. A year later the first fully-fledged colliery canteen in the Forest opened at Northern United, where soup, meat and vegetables, pudding and tea cost 1s. 3d.

If prices seem low it must be remembered that wages were very low. A soldier's pay was especially low, the wife of an army private received 17s. per week from the government, plus 5s. for the first child, 3s. for the second child, 2s. for athird child and 1s. each for any more. Her husband had to contribute 7s. from his pay, which left him with only 1s. per day.

There were all manner of restrictions and regulations, many of them necessary, but some merely petty, irksome and time consuming. There were also all manner of people given authority, many performed useful services but some were petty-minded, revelling in their new-found positions to the general annoyance of almost everybody else.

There were rumours of spies and enemy forces landing by parachutes. If now, from the distance of half a century, some of the following seems like a comedy, remember it was a comedy played against a grim background.

CHAPTER TWO

RECEPTION AREA

During the Munich crisis in September 1938, when war seemed imminent, the British Government published some hastily devised plans for the evacuation of London. Dulwich College, London, had already made its plans; a senior master, who knew the Forest of Dean and Littledean Guest House, had made arrangements for the staff and their wives, and the senior boys to be accommodated at the Guest House. The rest of the school would camp at the old fever hospital at Greenbottom just outside the village of Littledean.

On 26 September 1938 a preliminary party left Dulwich for Littledean, taking clothes, books, gas masks and enough food for two days. Those two days were spent preparing the hospital for its new inhabitants. On Wednesday 28 September the main party — three hundred boys — arrived, some by coaches, a few of the senior boys on bicycles, the majority by train. Unfortunately, those who came by train arrived too late to get a connection to Cinderford station and had to spend the night in a hall in Newnham.

A marquee had been erected at Greenbottom in which the evacuees had their meals; food was cooked by the wives of the masters. On Sunday some of the evacuees attended morning service at Littledean Church, others walked to the Wesleyan Chapel at Cinderford. On Monday some of the boys were taken down Princess Royal Colliery at Bream, on Tuesday a college team played a Lydney team at rugby — Lydney won. By then Neville Chamberlain had returned from his meeting with Hitler, waved his piece of paper at the cameras and declared, 'I believe it is peace for our time'. The evacuees went back to Dulwich.

On 31 August 1939 a wireless announcement said, 'It has been decided to start evacuation of school children and other priority

The WVS and WI played a vital role during the war.

classes as already arranged under the government scheme, tomorrow, Friday, 1 September.' Although the announcement was rather badly phrased, it was not people who had to be evacuated but the places where they lived, this time the evacuation scheme itself was better planned.

By the early part of 1939, Britain had been divided into areas known as 'evacuation', 'neutral', and 'reception'. The Forest of Dean was a reception area to which evacuees would be sent. Reception committees had been formed, drawing their members from district and parish councils, the WVS, Women's Institutes, religious organizations and the head teachers of schools. Parish reception and billeting officers had been appointed. Village schools or halls became reception centres. The WVS was in charge of the supply of communal meals and general welfare. Emergency rations were in store; Newnham, for example, had 196 tins of meat, 126 tins of unsweetened milk, 176 tins of sweetened milk, 185 lb of biscuits and 36½ lb of chocolate for a possible influx of 404 evacuees. Under the auspices of the district councils, volunteers had made diligent house-to-house checks of available accommodation for evacuees (see chart on page 16).

By June 1939, East Dean (chief billeting officer, Revd T.T. Haines) was told to expect 650 evacuees on the first day of evacuation and 800 on the second day. They would come by rail which would mean changing trains at Newnham for Cinderford station. Later when it was suggested that the evacuees would 'detrain' at Newnham, the clerk to East Dean Rural District Council (RDC) issued a warning that the East Dean Evacuation Committee would not be responsible for any confusion or trouble which might arise if evacuees from Birmingham were detrained at Newnham instead of Cinderford.

In the same month West Dean was told to expect 800 children: 400 going to Coleford, 150 to Lydbrook, 125 to Bream, 125 to Whitecroft. By October 1939, West Dean had received 60 unaccompanied children, 46 below school age, 30 mothers (with children) and 2 expectant mothers. Lydney District, by 15 September 1939, had received and billeted 291 unaccompanied schoolchildren and 254 other persons. At that time Lydney had the following emergency rations in store at the school in Church Road: 14 cases of corned beef, 30 cases of milk, 2 cases of chocolate and 47 cases of biscuits.

The majority of evacuees came from Birmingham, others from London, with lesser numbers from Surrey, Manchester and other places. 'We had a girl and a boy from Birmingham – at no small inconvenience to our family, Mum and Dad and my grandparents and me of course – and I had to give up my bedroom. An elder sister apparently worked at Cadbury's Bournville factory and every week without fail a parcel of chocolate rejects arrived by post, but although we shared our home with them, they never shared their chocolate with us.'

In early October 1939 a man from Sparkhill, Birmingham, wrote to complain:

> I visited my wife who is an evacuee at a place called Lydney
> in Gloucestershire and returned very dissatisfied. She is

Children from the Birmingham area were sent to the Forest of Dean.

living in a large room with an old woman and her three grandchildren. The old woman is 75 and therefore practically incapable. They are living in a large room, but there are not enough beds. In one corner the old woman sleeps with her three grandchildren and the bed is not large enough. In another bed sleeps four children and there is not enough room to turn over. . . . In another corner is a single bed and in it sleeps my two oldest boys (10 & 11). The floor is all cracked and on a cold day you can feel the cold striking up, it wants covering with oil cloth. There is hardly any covering on the beds.

Another letter arrived, this time from a man from Small Heath, Birmingham, who explained that his wife and children were billeted at Lydney (Pillowell actually), and were also not comfortable. Before anything could be done, another letter came to say that the man had fetched his family home. Apparently the son of the house in Lydney had been very objectionable. In the meantime the clerk to Lydney RDC had received a letter from Birmingham Council asking him to check the situation. Having done so, the clerk replied to the effect that the evacuee children had been ill-mannered and as their behaviour would have been unacceptable in a better type of home, it was the best that could be done for them.

Council clerks and their helpers had a great deal of extra work thrust upon them – some of it quite unnecessary. It was a very trying time all round. The evacuee children were torn from their homes, many spent weary hours in overcrowded trains, going to they knew not where. No wonder some of them wetted beds and were difficult to manage. Even well-groomed children could look rough on arrival, while those from deprived areas could look most unappealing. Some children arrived in summer clothing and with no provision for the colder months that lay ahead.

About thirty Birmingham children arrived at Brockweir Halt,

with gas-masks slung on their shoulders and a little case of clothes, otherwise just as they stood, all wore hats. They looked bewildered, some of them were obviously frightened. Several houses became very crowded and some of them were billeted in households where they were unused to children and in those days Brockweir did not have electricity or mains water. Evacuees came from London en famille, young fathers were in the forces, older men found work locally. Some of these Londoners said they'd never known such bliss as they found in Brockweir, which they described as idyllic, and after the war they remained in the village.

By the second week in September 1939 there were 138 evacuees billeted in West Dean and no complaints from the householders. All the evacuee expectant mothers had been transferred to Cheltenham. The West Dean RDC clerk reported that as a Receiving Authority, the council was only required to supply details to the Evacuation Authority and was not responsible for the collection of any monies, including enforced payments for billeted evacuees.

By November, 71 evacuee mothers and 112 children had come to Coleford, 65 mothers and 102 children had returned home, and 66 unaccompanied children had been received, 6 of whom had gone home. Of the 22 mothers and 37 children who had come, 8 mothers and 13 children had returned home. Out of 140 expectant mothers from Birmingham who had come to Gloucestershire, only 80 could be located two days later.

In October 1939 the police received instructions from the War Office to find billets for soldiers and they began to make arrangements for the billeting of 250 troops around Lydney. In response to this, Mr G. Spearing, clerk to Lydney RDC wrote to Mr R. Moon, clerk to Gloucestershire County Council, pointing out that there were approximately 350 schoolchildren from the Yardley Grammar School billeted in Lydney as well as 90 women and young children, and the committee therefore found it inconsistent with the Government [Evacuation] Scheme that troops should also be billeted. He concluded, 'Apart from this, I am to suggest that it is most undesirable that troops should be billeted where girl students are residing.'

Things did not always run smoothly for the evacuees or the residents of the Forest. During a hot, dry summer, the mother of an evacuee family living on St Briavels Common went to fetch water from the communal well and was told, 'This is our water, get back to the city where you belong'. An evacuee at Longhope was assaulted by her husband who accused her of consorting with other men. He was bound over for twelve months and fined £2. In another case, a woman living in a large house with spacious grounds not far from Ruardean said, 'I've got a big house, I'll have a dozen boys, I'm used to boys'. She was sent twelve girls.

In June 1940 West Dean District Council exercised its powers to make billeting of evacuees compulsory. The clerk said approximately 5,000 forms asking people to volunteer billets had been sent out, but less than 200 favourable replies had been received. There were receiving centres at Coleford, Bream, Whitecroft, and Lydbrook. (The Ministry of Health regarded Stowfield House as too large for the hostel accommodation required to be provided by the West Dean area. The 396 evacuees received in West Dean were billeted as follows: Bream 149, Pillowell and district 73, Coleford and district 174. It had been intended to allocate some to Lydbrook but it had nowhere large enough to accommodate a whole school group, which educational requirements stated should remain intact.

In the following month 1,400 more evacuees from Birmingham schools arrived and it proved difficult to find accommodation for them. In September there was a proposal to send another 2,000 evacuees. This influx of evacuees in 1940 was due to the heavy bombing suffered by London, Birmingham and other large towns. After experiencing this bombing, it took some children a long time to realize they were safe in the Forest. Some were so frightened that they were afraid to go outside for some time.

Another influx of evacuees came in 1944 because of the heavy raids on the south coast and London. These raids included V1 bombs, which were mechanical, unmanned and exploded on impact. These 'buzz bomb' raids started in mid-July 1944 and in September the V2 rocket raids started. The number of evacuees was not so large this time, however, and most of the children were billeted with families and absorbed into the local schools.

In June 1940 Lydney accommodated 244 evacuees at a few hours' notice. They were the 209 boys and 35 officers from the London County Council's training ship *Exmouth*, stationed at Burnham-on-Crouch. Mr Thompson, Chairman of Lydney RDC, expressed pleasure at their arrival, but added a warning that Lydney residents might want to get rid of the schoolchildren billeted on them and take the training ship's boys instead – 'They are all trained in housework and they will be a comparative asset to the householders,' he said.

In August 1940 a billeting fraud was heard at Coleford Court, the first case of its kind in the Forest. The defendant was accused of intent to defraud the Postmaster General of the sum of 6s. on three occasions. The Chairman of the Magistrates said the case was a serious one and on conviction the defendant could be sent to prison for six months and fined £100. However, the defendant was fined £2 on each charge and ordered to pay £2 2s. costs.

On the last day of 1940 the Drybrook Women's Institute entertained all the evacuee children of school age – about ninety of whom were from Birmingham.

The need was expressed for communal welfare centres, such as mothers' clubs, nursery centres and weekend hostels for visiting husbands.

In September 1941 a present was given to the matron at Stowfield House, who was leaving after fifteen months during which she had been in charge of a great many evacuee children from all parts of Britain. At the same time the WVS withdrew from the hostel. The chairman of West Dean RDC and the clerk declined to comment on the action of Lydbrook WVS in withdrawing their help.

In 1941 several evacuees returned home as they had in the first months of the war and parents were blamed for evacuee children leaving West Dean. In November of that year, however, more evacuees were expected at Lydney and another appeal was made to householders to provide suitable accommodation. By March 1942, evacuees again began drifting back home and the chairman of London County Council called for a halt to this.

Greenbottom Hospital near Littledean was being used as an emergency hospital for evacuee children suffering from minor skin troubles. In June 1942 a nurse visiting the hospital said she was horrified that a hospital should be allowed to get into such a state and asked for an enquiry.

At the end of 1942, the headmaster of a West Ham school said there was a shining example of the evacuation scheme in the Forest. He spoke of the happy results of West Ham children being billeted at Ruardean Hill School. In the first eighteen months no child had gone back to West Ham. 'In both Ruardeans the children could not have been more favourably or happily placed. It was a privilege and pleasure to work in the most cordial relationship with the local head teachers . . . appreciate the way local children in both villages received the West Hammers.'

Another note of appreciation of Forest hospitality had been received earlier in the year from the headmaster of Chingford County High School who had been recalled to Essex by its

Education Committee. He asked the clerk to West Dean Parish Council 'to convey to the Council my deep appreciation of the arrangements made and the facilities offered for evacuated pupils from this school in your area. I feel the Council and your householders who have received our children in the Coleford area have, generally speaking, done all they could for our pupils.'

Aston Commercial School came to Cinderford, and used the premises of East Dean Grammar School in the afternoons, but later the two schools were amalgamated. Mrs E. came in 1940 when she was thirteen:

> I'd never heard of the Forest of Dean before. A new school, new uniform, it was quite an adventure and of course, I was still with my Birmingham school friends which was a big help. And on Monday nights there was the Wesley Monday Guild when we were entertained by singing. Oh no, there were no difficulties, no unhappinesses.

From Bream Infant School Log Book:

6.9.39	School re-opened after summer holidays. Owing to a number of evacuee children being admitted the Registers were not marked all the rest of the week.
10.6.40	12 evacuees admitted from Rochford & Sutton, Essex, with teacher.
30.9.40	Admitted 12 evacuees.
23.5.41	School closed to receive evacuees from Filton.
26.5.41	14 evacuees from Filton admitted.
20.1.42	Heavy snowfall. Only 38% of children at school.
6.3.42	Another snowfall caused attendance to drop again.
13.6.42	The head teacher of all three schools given permission to visit Ruardean Hill School to see a scheme of feeding which has proved most successful. [The possibility of providing midday meals at Bream was under discussion.]
24.8.42	School officially re-opened. During holiday the

school was fitted with blackout curtains making it very dark and depressing.

5.1.43   The last official evacuees left to return to Southend.

20.9.43   Feeding in Schools Scheme put into operation.

14.2.44   3.15 p.m. Mrs B. brought a boy from the lowest class who had a piece of crayon lodged in his nose. Mrs B. took the child to Dr O. who lives next door to the school. He refused to look at the child and told her to bring him back to the evening surgery. In the evening the mother sent to inform me that the child had sneezed the crayon down.

4.9.44   The Head Teacher of the Girls' Department had letter from Gloucester informing her that all evacuees were to be placed on the Evacuation Register.

18.9.44   Sylvia and Jean I. have been transferred from the Evacuation Register as their mother, a war widow, does not intend to return to London.

At Drybrook, evacuee pupils were taught at the Village Hall until the end of July 1941. Then they merged with Drybrook School. Most came from Birmingham, but some from London.

The first evacuees in Newland arrived on 12 September 1939. They were from London initially and later from Bristol, Essex and South Wales. Most had returned by early 1942.

Five Acres had evacuees from London, Glasgow, East Ham, Kent, Eastbourne, Barking, Bristol, Coventry, Bath, and Surrey.

At Parkend the evacuees came from Surrey, Swansea, Bristol, Birmingham, Eastbourne, Middlesex, Sussex, but mainly from Essex in June 1940.

In Lydbrook most evacuees started arriving in June 1940 from Essex, Birmingham, Surrey, Eastbourne, London – and then from Bristol in 1941. At Ellwood and Lane End, Coleford, they came from London, Essex and Surrey. The vast majority in Bream came from Essex.

'Evacuees to Newnham came from Birmingham. These were

GOVERNMENT EVACUATION SCHEME
(Ministry of Health)

	LYDNEY RURAL DISTRICT	EAST DEAN RURAL DISTRICT	WEST DEAN RURAL DISTRICT	NEWNHAM PARISH
TOTAL NUMBER OF HABITABLE ROOMS	12,391	18,504	21,293	1,296
TOTAL NUMBER OF ADDITIONAL PERSONS WHO COULD BE ACCOMMODATED	3,884	5,008	5,214	404
UNACCOMPANIED CHILDREN	1,043	1,883	1,963	169
TEACHERS AND HELPERS	63	167	322	34
OTHERS	1,007	958	1,771	72
ACCOMMODATION RESERVED PRIVATELY	1,079	1,915	1,004	184
TOTAL	3,192	4,923	5,060	459
ADDITIONAL BEDDING REQUIRED — MATTRESSES DOUBLE	261	431	925	
MATTRESSES SINGLE	256	868	850	20
BLANKETS DOUBLE	780	958	1834	66
BLANKETS SINGLE	742	1,820	1718	

Details and figures from the Government Evacuation Scheme (Ministry of Health) for the Forest area.

children from much poorer parents and those who "took them in" said they came from "another world". Their personal hygiene and habits left much to be desired. Most of them were back in Birmingham within six months.'

The majority of evacuees at Bilson School came from Birmingham as did those at Double View, St Whites, Steam Mills and Joys Green School. At Viney Hill School they came from Eastbourne, Essex and Bristol.

At Lydney Grammar School the Lydney pupils used the school premises in the mornings and the Yardley Grammar School (Birmingham) pupils in the afternoons from September 1939 for about six months or so, at which stage the evacuees began to trickle back home. Those that remained joined Lydney Grammar School on a more permanent basis.

Children were billeted in several of the big houses in the Forest:

At Bradley Court, Mitcheldean – a girls' school from Kent
At Flaxley Abbey – St Felix School for boys
At Huntley Manor – St Christopher's Home, for children from broken homes who were under school age
At Lydney Park – North Foreland School (pupils from Yardley Grammar School were billeted at houses in Lydney)
Oaklands, Newnham – a school
St Briavels Lodge – a hostel for evacuees from Bristol

From the beginning, the Government had promised to pay an allowance to householders who had evacuees but it was not until mid–September 1939 that it was made clear that parents of evacuee children would be expected to make a contribution towards the allowances. And another two weeks passed before the terms (which included a means test) were announced.

The billetor received 10s. 6d. for the first child, 8s. 6d. per child if more than one – this was to cover full board and lodgings. For mothers and infants the billetor was only expected to provide lodgings, for which they received 5s. per adult and 3s. per child.

CHAPTER THREE

ARP, AFS, WVS AND BOMBS

The Air Raid Precaution (ARP) Act was passed at the end of 1937. It took the form of a free issue of gas masks for everyone (ordinary civilian gas masks were being made at a cost of 2s. 6d. each in May 1937), the provision of bomb-proof shelters, the formation of decontamination squads to deal with mustard and other liquid gases, instructions on making refuge rooms gas-proof and special fire-fighting equipment. It also included the recruitment of air-raid wardens, first-aid and rescue services. After the Munich crisis in 1938, ARP gathered momentum and at the outbreak of war about two and a half million people had enrolled in civil defence – as ambulance men, fire-fighters, rescue workers and wardens.

Fire Schemes Regulations were introduced in 1938 and any fit man of more than twenty-five years was eligible for the Auxiliary Fire Service (AFS). By 1940 there was an urgent need for more firemen and in 1941 any man over thirty, whether or not registered for army service, could volunteer to join the AFS for full-time duty instead of the Armed Forces provided he had not been medically examined or in a reserved occupation. Men accepted would not be called up and would receive £3 5s. per week and a uniform. However, by February 1941 West Dean had not got an AFS but there was now a proposal that Coleford should have an AFS Scheme.

Meanwhile the police and the defence services were combining in the fight against incendiaries. In the agricultural area around the Forest incendiary bombs presented a danger to

Parkend Fire Service.

ripening corn, and farmers and their workers, Civil Defence, Home Guard and ordinary residents formed fire watches for the harvest fields. Miners and other workers served as part-time firemen too. One miner-cum-fireman said:

> We paraded on Sunday mornings in Cinderford – a lot of nonsense. I was only ever called out to one real fire. It was a barn on fire at Mitcheldean. I went up a ladder on one side, my mate on the other side of the barn. I got going with my hose and knocked my mate clean off his ladder. Still, it could have been worse, he could have knocked me off.

To practise their hose drill the AFS was employed at Newnham to blow out rooks' nests from the trees along Whetstone Brook. However, many of Cinderford's fire servicemen did see real service and by May 1942 they had fought several fires caused by bomb attacks outside the Forest. When London was hard-hit by flying bombs in 1944, for several

WVS volunteers with a field kitchen somewhere in the Forest.

weeks Forest Civil Defence Volunteers went to Gloucester station on Sunday mornings to get the London train in order to relieve their hard-pressed comrades.

The Women's Voluntary Service (WVS) for Civil Defence (CD) was formed in 1938 originally to encourage women to enrol in ARP services; its scope was later extended. Members had to pay for their uniforms – green tweed suit and beret or felt hat. They looked very respectable and very middle-class. As initially they were very middle-class they ran the risk of becoming just another bossy middle-class organization, but instead they became a very valuable service, overseeing the welfare of evacuees and troops, running British Restaurants – indeed, extending their duties to almost any emergency.

'What's that uniform, what does she do?' asked a refugee, on seeing a formidable, middle-aged familiar figure in the Forest.

'She's a member of the Women's Voluntary Service.'

'Oh,' after a slight pause, 'I'd rather pay and have a younger one.'

There was a scheme to have a British Restaurant in the Forest. A letter appeared in the weekly paper, the writer complaining of the local authority's reluctance to proceed with the scheme and giving the menu of one he had recently visited: roast beef, Yorkshire pudding, two vegetables, steamed pudding with custard, bread, butter and cheese, three biscuits, cup of tea – all for 1s. 6d., and cooked by the WVS. But Cinderford never got a British Restaurant.

The question of establishing a British Restaurant at Coleford was raised by one district councillor, but his main reason for it appears to have been so that the councillors could have food when they came to the town for meetings.

At a meeting held on 30 June 1939, it was stated that there was definite evidence of progress in ARP organization in the Forest. Lydney and Cinderford, but not Coleford, were to have report centres for ARP. Messages about air raids would be sent to a report centre and from there to the control centre at Gloucester. The basement of St Annal's Institute at Cinderford had been commandeered and would be equipped at a cost of about £70. At Lydney the Highway Office in Forest Road would take little to make it ready.

The first meeting of the West Dean Civil Defence Committee was held on 17 July 1939. Officers were appointed to deal with casualties, decontamination, rescue, demolition and ambulance. There was an outline report on the Evacuation Scheme in West Dean and the clerk suggested there should be more publicity about the August Blackout (this was a rehearsal for the real thing which began on 1 September). Another meeting was held on 11 September when the allocation of evacuees was discussed. A letter from the WVS suggested:

1. Visiting all evacuee mothers and children to see if they were content.
2. Helping them to keep in touch with parents and relatives.
3. Making arrangements re. clothing and other necessities.

At the October meeting anti-gas training for council staff, and waste paper collections were discussed; at the November meeting

The Forest of Dean Civil Defence Heavy Rescue teams, 1943.

first-aid was on the agenda including first-aid classes at Lydbrook, a first-aid and warden's post at Bream, and a first-aid post and clinic at Coleford. Twelve months later a proposal was put forward for public shelters in High Street, Newland Street, and Market Place, Coleford, which would provide protection for three hundred people. More air-raid shelters were needed and in Lydney area people were providing their own. At Woolaston people decided to build a shelter in Nupend Farm dingle by using corrugated iron covered by a foot of earth and supported by timbers over the ditch. The erection of the shelter was overseen by a First World War veteran.

In June 1940 men in East Dean were leaving ARP for the Local Defence Volunteer (LDV) force, which had a greater attraction. And Lydney RDC received a complaint that 'Lydney is not defended in any shape or form against possible air raids'. The council felt that more members were needed for both ARP and LDV.

The Forest of Dean mobile ARP unit, Belle Vue Road, Cinderford, *c.* 1941.

Lydney CD Committee complained it was all Home Guard and no ARP and by September 1942 no Civil Defence transfers to the Home Guard were allowed. Next month Cinderford came second in the county ARP service competition, scoring 89 marks. Filton came first with 93.

In December 1942 there was a suggestion at the CD Committee that all defence services, including the Home Guard, should be combined. A month later West Dean decided to take disciplinary action against 'ARP slackers' – estimated at less than 5 per cent of total membership. In 1943 Civil Defence work became compulsory.

In the spring of 1941 there was 'trouble down at t'post', or as the newspaper put it, 'friction' among the wardens at Sedbury ARP post. Although we are not told details about the 'friction', apparently the cause of the trouble was the condition of the post itself, which was said to be very damp and unfit to stay in. The Lydney district surveyor said ARP posts were like clubs, a remark hardly likely to improve tempers down at the Sedbury post. Matters could not have been made better when a regional commissioner stated that warden's posts were 'too good and their costs too high'.

At a meeting of the Lydney CD Committee, provisions for dealing with air-raid casualties were discussed. A letter from the Ministry of Home Security stated that civilian gas masks did not give full protection from ammonia. Councillor F. Virgo said many people were wearing gas masks while peeling onions for pickling.

From time to time the public was told always to carry gas masks, but after a few months many people did not carry them, although it was said to be illegal not to do so. In June 1940 there were rumours of a new gas, 'arsine', which was said to penetrate gas masks and every mask was fitted with an additional filter. Fortunately gas was not used.

An ARP exercise at St Briavels brought a charge of 'amateurish', together with an accusation of polluting a water supply, from a man serving in the RAF. Woolaston complained that it could not hear a siren and was told it could not have its own siren. Some people in other places complained because they could hear a siren – sirens did make an awesome noise. A small evacuee boy was reassured by a Forest warden, 'They're only testing it out.' The boy retorted, 'Where I come from, they're wearing it out.'

Newnham decided to buy an air-raid siren and to have a house-to-house collection to help with the cost. 'Silly old greyheads,' said a recently arrived young evacuee from Bristol where there had been very heavy bombing.

'Yes,' said a miner, 'you could stand on St Annal's tump o'nights and see Bristol all afire.'

An evacuee at St Briavels said that one Sunday night when Bristol was raided you could almost read the paper in the light from the blaze.

In July 1940 this advice was published in the Forest newspapers:

Don't phone after air raids. If an air raid warning has been sounded or if an air raid has taken place in your district do not use the telephone or send telegrams, stated the Minister of Home Security. These services are needed for defence purposes until a considerable time after raiders have passed.

So your phone call might hinder the saving of somebody's life or the putting out of a fire. Similarly the public must refrain, during such periods, from telephoning or telegraphing to places which they believe to have been bombed.

Bombs did fall over the Forest but there was no loss of human life as far as I can ascertain. The following list gives brief details of bombs that fell in the area:

Three by the brickworks at Coleford, which landed in clay and made very little impression.

Four by Northern United Colliery at 10 p.m. one night, just at change of shift, leaving only small craters and no one hurt.

One bomb dropped on a beech tree by the side of a house at Wigpool, killing a dog.

One bomb at the Causeway, Cinderford – no damage.

Two on a Sunday night at Bishopswood – no damage.

'S.H. was standing at Drybrook Cross with the policeman and heard aeroplanes. The policeman said "It's some of ours". Then they heard a whistling noise and five bombs dropped in the clay on Steam Mills Green. It was said the bombs were heard underground at Northern United.

'S.H. with his mother and father were at the back door of his house one night when it was raining heavily and they heard the aeroplanes which dropped several bombs near the Lea Line Tunnel but did no damage.'

Just outside St Briavels a bomb dropped and there was still no vegetation on that spot in 1995.

Several bombs dropped in a line near Bream, none of which exploded and a bomb disposal squad came and stopped for quite a while and camped out in a barn.

A bomb fell at Whitecroft close to the pin factory and another fell at Gill House Farm on the Chepstow Road and blew the windows out of all the cottages around.

There were several bombs at Tidenham on both sides of the A48.

'The engines of enemy planes could be heard surging . . . following up the river. It was sporadic bombing, not intentional, but jettisoned.'

A number of bombs, including incendiaries – they were flaring in the sky as they dropped – and oil bombs fell in various places. Elsewhere there was, ten feet deep, an unexploded bomb; several other high explosives and incendiary bombs resulted in the death of two cattle and a hedge fire.

An unexploded land mine caused a temporary evacuation at Broadwell: 'My mother carried me away in one arm and a bag of threepenny bits in the other.'

Bombs dropped behind Woolaston council houses, Priors Mesne near Touchway Bay at Hewelsfield; six or more high explosive bombs straddled the South Wales railway line – 'that would be in 1940 or '41, that's when we had the bombs'.

Bombs fell at Monk Hill Farm in the parish of Flaxley on two successive nights in July 1941. On the first night one made the conventional crater, the other made a considerable tump. Some time later the farmer had a cow die which he put in the crater and took about a dozen dung cart loads from the tump to cover the dead cow, thus levelling the tump. Today the site of the tump is still level, the ground has not sunk in any way and yet there must be a hollow beneath the surface. An explanation eludes all those who know of the incident.

The bomb that partially destroyed the bridge over the Longhope Brook at Blaisdon also caused a rift between two neighbours who lived right by the bridge. One woman said to the other, 'If you hadn't been having a fag out in your garden we'd never have had that bomb.' They never spoke to each other again.

Bombs fell in Westbury parish, Newnham parish and no doubt in several other parishes not mentioned above.

The Forest escaped very lightly, there were no air raids on the scale that many towns experienced. Despite the claims made to the contrary, the raiders were not really interested in the Forest. Most bombs in the Forest were dropped by mistake or because a searchlight had picked out the bombers or a fighter plane had spotted them. But this will be hotly contested by some, by those who think that bombing was more accurate than it really was, and that the bombers were after the railway lines in the Forest which carried munitions – the Hereford–Gloucester single line 'full of trains carrying ammunition to or from Hereford' and so forth. By the time that much of the Forest had become a veritable arsenal very few, if any, bombs fell in the Forest.

One day a barrage balloon with a dangling wire drifted over Cinderford from the Bristol direction, and was later shot down over some woods near Drybrook.

At the end of September 1939 a National Registration census was held and soon afterwards everyone was issued with an identity card, containing the person's name, address and National

At the end of 1939 everyone was issued with an identity card. It was an offence not to have the card with you at all times.

Littledean Ambulance Class, 1941.

Registration number. This was supposed to be carried at all times. In July 1944 at Coleford Police Court a twenty-eight-year-old woman was fined £1 for failing to carry and produce her identity card. This was the first case of its kind in the Forest.

The Littledean and Cinderford Ambulance Classes won awards. In February 1943 an ambulance man found a man living in a shack in a hole near Steam Mills. The man had been living as a hermit in the relics of old pit workings at The Folly. In a gap five yards across and three yards deep he had made a shack about four feet wide which resembled a hen coop. His bed was composed of wood and old sacking, for cooking he had a small oil stove, and for lighting a candle in a jam jar. The man was in a very poor state; there was four feet of water around the hole and almost up to the shack. It took two hours to get him out.

Almost a year earlier Dr Selby of Newnham (an ambulance class instructor) made a public plea for an ambulance for East Dean. It is almost unbelievable that in April 1942 East Dean had no ambulance, especially considering all the defence, casualty and rescue services. This deficiency resulted in letters in the local paper and the (temporary) resignation of a prominent councillor.

At one first-aid class, a member had just bandaged a man 'head to foot, he looked like a mummy', when someone shouted 'it's nine o'clock and your young man [a soldier] is waiting for you'. The first-aider said that she, 'left hurriedly, leaving my patient still bound – I suppose someone eventually released him.'

At a first-aid exam a woman unable to answer any questions said, 'I can't think, my brains is addled today'. And at a first-aid exercise in a riverside village a 'casualty' found on a seat on the green, who growled 'Go away, you buggers', was soon found to be not one of the exercise casualties but a casualty of alcohol.

Not many people in those days had telephones, not even the air-raid wardens. At the first air-raid warning wardens in this riverside village had to go up to the yew tree and wait for the all clear – they thought they would hear from the telephone kiosk. They were there all night and were heard swearing horribly in the morning.

In October 1944 Civil Defence Duty was relaxed and finally stood down in the following May.

Mitcheldean Special Constables.

CHAPTER FOUR

THEY CAN'T BLACKOUT THE MOON

It was a popular song of the time – 'Who cares if we're without a light? They can't blackout the moon'. But most people did care, the blackout was the cause of more grumbling than any other restriction or inconvenience during the war. The blackout started on 1 September 1939, imposed under Defence Regulation No. 24. The public was encouraged to eat plenty of carrots as an aid to good sight in the dark.

If even a chink of light showed it was an offence; householders had to buy blackout material, blinds or curtains if they could be found. The headlights of motor vehicles had to be masked and in the new year a special headlight mask with a narrow horizontal slit became compulsory. Even hand torches had to be masked. 'Put that light out!' became a familiar command. Officious wardens had the time of their lives and so did Special Constables. Soon there was a proliferation of Specials in every village, often a dozen or more attached to a police station. In April 1940 Forest Specials were complaining because they had no uniform. But soon uniformed Specials became a familiar sight. They patrolled the streets and lanes; some were sent to guard the Severn Railway Bridge, armed only with truncheons. Some set out to catch spies, and were greeted by, 'Hello, playing policemen again?' More than one police station became a kind of clubhouse where quoits was the favourite pastime.

Failure to 'blackout' effectively became one of the two most frequent offences in the Forest. Week after week, month after month, year after year, offenders appeared at the three Forest

'They can't blackout the moon' was a popular song at a time when blackout regulations meant that all man-made light, at least, had to be blacked out.

police courts. House lights, vehicle lights, fires, including a colliery stack at Clements End – almost any light that could be seen out of doors was good for an appearance at court. Roof lights were often forgotten about, but not by wardens and Specials. In March 1940 five people were fined 5s. each at Coleford for this omission.

A Steam Mills man was fined £1 3s. costs for permitting a light to shine from a bedroom. The Special Constable said the defendant had used 'extreme bad language'. A month later, Mrs R., accused of showing a light, was 'very abusive' to a Special Sergeant.

A Special at Newnham was:

very hot on the blackout . . . if he stood at an angle of 37½° he could see a line of light three-quarters of an inch wide down the side of the window. Just the thing an enemy bomber would be looking for . . . looking back . . . it was just a load of crap. A river of moonlight was far more important than a chink of light.

But they couldn't blackout the moon.

In March 1941 a large crop of Berry Hill offences was heard at Coleford Court and Edwin G. of Stowe had had the effrontery to have a bonfire. In October of that year a miner was killed by a motor cycle during the blackout at Hangerberry Hill. And two months later twenty-five people were fined 10s. each at Littledean for using unscreened hand torches. The Chairman of the Bench said the offences were very serious and had to be stopped. 'A serious offence' became a stock phrase with all chairmen of magistrates in the Forest.

When a youth started flashing a torch when the pub closed, the burly St Briavels constable told him, 'Now look here, I'm not taking you to Coleford, I've better things to do, but if I ever catch you again. . . .'

On 17 September 1944 blackout ended and was replaced by a 'dim-out'. Headlights were unmasked the following February.

The matter of the blackout was further confused because, on occasions, if you didn't show a light you could be summoned for not showing a light. After going through the Forest wartime newspapers I am convinced that riding bicycles without lights in the dark was the most popular occupation in the Forest of Dean.

Special Constables and Civil Defence members at Newnham.

It even surpassed showing lights; it was a steady, regular offence as the number of fines at Forest courts proved.

Like so much else during the war, batteries for bicycle lamps were difficult to obtain. Their life could be prolonged, however, by warming them up in the oven. This did not give them a much longer life though, and it was a trick that could only be done a couple of times to a battery. There were also acetylene lamps. One miner who was also a fireman was called out unexpectedly one night — as it was summer his acetylene lamp was not on his bicycle. He was caught riding lightless to the emergency by a policeman and taken to Littledean Court. A mistake had been made about the night the offence had occurred, so he pleaded not guilty and was fined 5s. He handed the police sergeant a 10s. note and was given change for £1. There were also oil lights for bicycles, but these could cause a conflagration.

In June 1940 G.W. of Abenhall was fined 15s. and 2s. 6d. costs for having no lights on his bicycle. When challenged by Special Constable W.T., he said, 'I suppose you are out for a stripe'. At the same time F.H. of Lydney was fined 35s. for driving a car exceeding 20 m.p.h. through Westbury and Newnham, and also for failing to have white paint on the car bumpers and running boards. (A speed limit of 20 m.p.h. in built-up areas was introduced in February 1940.)

Turn the pages of the Forest newspapers during the war and with regular monotony there appears 'No lights on bicycle', 'No lights on bicycle' and of course 'lights showing'. A man living in Newnham provided a bit of a change, 'fined 15s. for driving a car without lights'. In any case, such light that was allowed wasn't much help, moonlight was much better, and the Foresters became adept at riding bicycles without lights.

But none of this explains the popularity of riding bicycles without lights. Scores, no hundreds of people were fined for the offence but it had little or no deterrent effect. For everyone who was caught there must have been a dozen or more who were not — I for one was never caught although I used to ride lampless o' nights to and from the cinema at Cinderford, but I used to get a little apprehensive when riding through Littledean and past the

Littledean Special Constables.

gaol. Maybe we youngsters did it for the fun of it and older people to show their Forest independence. Anyway, it gave all those Specials something to do, but I can't help wondering why police and magistrates hadn't something better to do, like the burly constable at St Briavels.

Double Summer Time was introduced in 1941. A letter written by Richard Kear of Oldcroft, near Lydney, appeared in the *Forest Newspapers* in August and summed up the feelings of many people:

> . . . of all the senseless propositions to assist the war (and there are many) Double Summer Time has caused more swearing, more bad feeling, more anxiety for the children, more inconvenience for adults than anything else . . .

They couldn't blackout the moon, neither could they make the sun rise earlier or set later but they did fool some of the people some of the time.

CHAPTER FIVE

RATIONING

Ration books for food had been ready since 1938 but were not issued until the end of September 1939. In November the imminent rationing of butter and bacon was announced and consumers were told to register with their chosen retailers before 23 November. Eventually the Government announced that rationing would begin on 8 January 1940. The allowance was to be 4 oz butter and 4 oz bacon per person, per week. Sugar and meat rationing followed and later other foodstuffs. Cheese was not rationed until May 1941. The allowances varied from time to time but this table gives the maximum and minimum per person, per week:

	Minimum	Maximum
Meat	1s. worth	2s. 2d. worth
Bacon	4 oz	8 oz
Cheese	1 oz	8 oz
Fat	1 oz	8 oz
Eggs	1/2	2
Tea	2 oz	4 oz
Sugar	8 oz	16 oz

Later in the war, 'Emergency Rations' were kept ready to be distributed in the Forest should they be needed. They were only to be used upon a call to 'action stations' or as directed by the Food Officer. These rations consisted of:

Per person: 7½ lb Biscuits, 24 oz Canned Corned Beef, 1 lb Baked Beans, 1 lb Sugar, 7½ oz Condensed Milk, 7 oz Margarine, 4 oz Tea, packed in hermetically-sealed tins

FOOD IS A MUNITION OF WAR

There's more in them than meets the eye

There's a change in the greengrocer's shop. We *do* regret the vanished piles of imported fruits. But shipping is needed for other things, so we turn to home-grown products which, fortunately, are plentiful and very good.

Carrots and potatoes, for instance. Dull and ordinary? Not a bit of it, when you know what wonderful things they do for you and the countless attractive ways in which they can be served.

Carrots and Potatoes fill many needs

Take carrots. Did you know that carrots contain sugar — just as fruits do? Eaten raw, they take the place of apples and children love them this way.

Carrots also protect against infection, especially against colds, and — it sounds almost magical — help you to see in the dark. And, ladies! carrots are splendid for the complexion.

Now, what's so interesting about potatoes? Well, potatoes are a grand energy food. They are warming, and very satisfying, and they, also, protect against illness.

Potatoes are nôt fattening. You could eat potatoes at every meal without putting on unwanted weight, and you probably would need less bread — which would save valuable shipping space. And potatoes help to keep your digestive system in order . . . a lot for your money in potatoes, isn't there?

So don't let us worry too much about what we *can't* get at the greengrocers.

WE'RE IN THE NEWS AND ON THE AIR

Food Facts announcements in the newspapers and Kitchen Front Talks on the wireless at 8.15 on weekday mornings

People were encouraged to eat more home-grown produce to compensate for the lack of imported foods.

and costing ten shillings. To be retained by consumer as a last resort should the area be cut off from supplies.

A system known as 'points rationing' was introduced in June 1941 (following the German example). Certain foods, such as jam, marmalade, and some tinned food, were given a points value, and each person had sixteen points per week. As the months passed more foods were added to the list: tinned meat, fish and vegetables; dried fruit; rice, sago and tapioca; condensed milk; breakfast cereals; syrup and treacle; and finally, in August 1942, biscuits.

In June 1941 clothes rationing started, soap was rationed in February 1942 with an allowance of 1 lb every four weeks.

Chocolate and sweets were rationed in July 1942, with an allowance of 8 oz every four weeks, later raised to 12 oz. Bread was not rationed during the war.

Soon after the war started petrol was rationed. Every motorist received a basic ration according to the size of the vehicle (a Ford Eight – five gallons per month), and a supplementary allowance could be obtained for essential business or domestic purposes. The latter included church attendance. In March 1942 the basic allowance was abolished, but this had no real impact in the Forest as very few Foresters had motor cars in those days. Those who were allowed petrol for essential business were liable to be stopped and asked if their journey really was essential business. Many more farmers acquired trailers to attach to their cars and some of them suddenly found it essential to transport boltens of straw or other farm produce along routes which took them past their favourite public house.

During the first months of the war the retail price of beer per pint (IPA) was 9d. in the smokeroom and 8d. in the public bar. As the war continued, beer became dearer (because it was more heavily taxed), weaker, and scarcer, although it was never rationed. 'It seems,' said my father, slapping a bag of malting barley which had just been threshed, 'that beer's as important as food.' During the times when beer was scarce, public houses were often closed or only open for a short time. In August 1942 *A Hint to Landlords* was published:

> I think it would be an excellent plan if landlords in every town and village in the Forest worked out a plan for opening . . . many hours barred against customers . . . easier if all decided to open, say, at 8.30 or 9 every evening . . .

Earlier that year West Dean Parish Council was concerned about the shortage of whisky. One headline read: 'Whisky as medicine, people are suffering unnecessarily as a result of the shortage.' The clerk was instructed to take the matter up with Mr Morgan Philips Price, MP.

In January 1940 Cinderford Co-op was appealing to customers regarding Meat Registration: 'If you have not registered, do so

Dried eggs – promoted by the Ministry of Food as a good substitute to the real thing.

immediately, otherwise your supply will not be guaranteed.' In March a man in West Dean said he had not been able to get any meat from his butcher since Christmas.

In April West Dean Food Committee received a letter from two milk retailers at Yorkley, who reported another milk retailer for 'undercutting' by selling milk at 6d. instead of 7d. per quart. A complaint was made that the meat at Coleford was 'not fit for dogs', which brought a reply from the West and East Dean Butchers' Associations. The public was urged to bring all its farthings into circulation as they were needed under the present system of rationing.

In July 1940 a Viney Hill man was fined £1 10s. and £1 16s. 6d. costs at Coleford for three offences connected with the illegal slaughter and sale of a pig (under the Livestock (Restriction of Slaughtering) Order, 1940). This was believed to be the first case of this description to come before the court.

A pig could be legally killed by or for private persons by applying to and obtaining a licence from the Food Officer. Then fourteen days' notice of the date of slaughter had to be given. Two pigs could be killed in a year but the bacon ration had to be surrendered. 'Pig Clubs' were formed and many families fed 'a pig for the house' but this had always been a custom in the Forest. Three hundred licences were issued in West Dean in one month.

Hard on the illegal pig case at Coleford came a similar one concerning bacon at Lydney Court where the offender was 'let off lightly' with a fine of £1 plus £1 1s. costs. These were not the only cases of illegal slaughtering and selling of meat. The following accounts show that some people did get away with it:

'They've caught you at last over your pig game.'

'Ah, but they weren't so clever as they thought they was. They saw two sides hanging up and did me for one pig, but 'twas two left sides hanging up there.'

'We went over to Drybrook to get a bit o' bacon on the side. It were fat bacon and we had parcels of it done up in newspaper under our arms, me and my mate. Well, there we was waitin' for the buzz, which wasn't due for some time, when along comes the bobby. He stops and talks and talks, in no hurry to move away. Well, 'twas a warmish evening and the fat from the bacon began to run. It began to run from me too, with the bobby standing there. Anyway the fat begins to seep through the paper and the bobby looks at the parcels and I began to sweat more than ever. We're for it now I think. And then the bobby says to us, "You want to get off home with that bacon afore it all runs away."'

Early in 1941 there was more trouble over meat. An allegation was made that people in West Dean were being deceived by retailers in the Forest over the sale of meat. At the end of February the Ministry of Food announced that the meat ration would be reduced from 1s. 2d. per week to 1s. per week; the

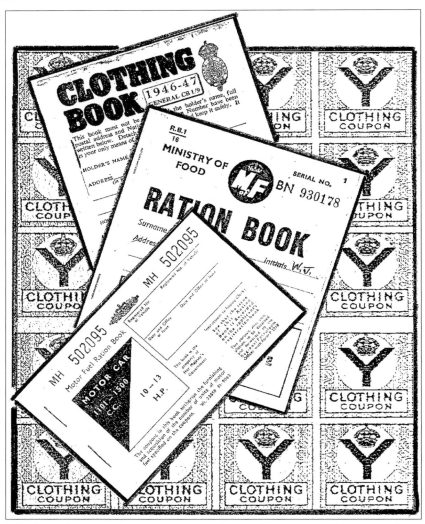

Clothing and motor fuel were rationed as well as food; coupons could be collected to help cover the cost of new items.

ration for a young child from 7*d*. to 6*d*. This was due to a reduction in home-produced stock coming forward for slaughter.

Cheese was allocated to districts before the decision to ration it and West Dean's allocation, due to increased population, was increased by 15 per cent. But the Forest MP was still pressing for an extra allocation for the Forest. Then the Ministry of Food announced that cheese was to be rationed. Farmworkers, miners and perhaps certain railway workers would have an extra allowance – mainly because of their lack of canteen facilities.

In July 1942 the West Dean Food Officer stated that twenty thousand new ration books had been delivered but few people had bothered to re-register. He warned that failure to re-register would leave them without food. Later a woman applied to change her retailer because the bacon was cut 'too thick'. The West Dean Food Committee considered her request 'trivial and paltry'.

At the end of the year a Cinderford trader was fined £60. He had been convicted on fourteen out of eighteen charges. His offences consisted of accepting clothing coupons that were not valid until a later date and of having had a child's supplementary ration book which did not bear the name and address of the holder. Early in 1943 a Westbury grocer was fined over £13 because he had omitted to cancel some food coupons. The Board of Trade employed snoopers who practised little tricks in order to catch traders evading regulations, although often these apparent evasions were not deliberate.

CHAPTER SIX

THEY CAME TO THE
FOREST

Almost as soon as the war started military personnel began arriving in the Forest:

On a Saturday afternoon in September 1939, I was picking Blaisdon plums in my Uncle's garden at Nailbridge, when a train came by and I saw all these sailors sitting in the carriages. (Mr Hale)

About twenty of these sailors came to Drybrook, all oldish men. They were billeted at the New Inn (now Hearts of Oak). Their job was guarding the ammo being stored in the old railway tunnel. Trains were coming twice a day with the stuff — we always thought it were torpedoes or sea mines. They had a guard house on top of the quarry which overlooked the tunnel, but they spent most of their time in the pubs. (Mr Hopkins)

The sailors came first, then the soldiers. They took over the Sunday school premises for accommodation. They came on the Sunday morning when the service was being held at our Methodist Chapel. (Mr Harris)

Units from the Royal Engineers, the Royal Army Ordnance Corps, the Royal Army Service Corps and the Pioneer Corps came to the Forest. Others came to man searchlights.

Members of Forestry Company 129 Royal Engineers, 1942.

There were searchlights in Oak Field on Littledean Hill and next to Colliers Court. They had generators by the old mine at St Annals. A bomb dropped by the Causeway. Mother used to have a few soldiers in on Saturday nights and give them faggots. The rugby ground was full of army huts, and Oak Field and Cinderford Town Football ground. The officers' mess was in a field next to Colliers Court. (Mr Warren)

There were Royal Engineers in Nissen huts opposite the White Hart at Ruspidge, some were billeted in the classrooms behind the Primitive Methodist Chapel in Church Road, and the officers were at the White Hart. The Engineers were engaged in felling and sawing timber, the Pioneers acted as their labourers. The Royal Army Ordnance Corps were helping store ammunition in the woods.

Searchlights were installed at strategic points near the Severn and the Wye. Soldiers were billeted in St Briavels Castle, and members of the Royal Air Force in the Crown at St Briavels. They had an Observer Post on the Common.

The Forestry Company 131 RE came to Broadwell in October 1940. Four sections of the Company were billeted in the Crown at Coalway and at two other local pubs. Others were billeted at Broadwell Memorial Hall. Officers were billeted at Whitecliff; one house there became the officers' mess and living quarters, another became the medical centre. Part of Wynolls House was used as offices and the sergeants' mess.

Mr Lander remembers:

The boys complained that there wasn't much entertainment in the district. So on Saturday nights we cleared the Hall of all the beds and kit and held dances in there. The dances became very popular, girls came to meet the soldiers. When it was well established ENSA came one night a month.

The Service Corps had a Motor Transport Section at Five Acres. They had two huts, one for sleeping quarters for the drivers and one for motor repairs and spares. Altogether there was about one hundred and forty troops. . . . We had trained tree fellers and sawyers. The first piece we felled was opposite Yew Tree Brake, mostly oak and beech, for pit props, a lot went to South Wales. We took bigger timber out of woods behind Brierley and Sallet Vallets, that was sawn and sent off for railway sleepers.

Pioneers were labouring for the Engineers at this time – they were living in huts at Coalway. After the Pioneers, in late '41 or early '42, Italian Prisoners of War did the labouring under the supervision of a Pioneer Company.

Our first sawmill was built at Cannop Crossroads, the second towards Lydbrook at Speculation and the third, which was driven by steam, was at Brierley.

In January 1943 the Coleford WVS gave a Christmas party for 300 troops stationed in the district. The meal consisted of several courses, including Christmas pudding and mince pies. One wonders where or how the WVS managed to get hold of all that food.

Minelifting Demonstration Section on Cinderford Recreational Ground, June 1943.

In July 1944 this Company of Royal Engineers left the Forest and went to France to fell timber in Normandy.

An Anti-Aircraft Unit that had been stationed at the top of High Nash left in 1941.

A Company of the Royal Army Ordnance Corps was stationed at Broadwell for a short time. They were storing ammunition in the Forest until the Americans came and took over.

CHAPTER SEVEN

MEN AND ARMOUR

Soon after the war started there was a suggestion that bands of civilians should be raised to resist invasion but nothing was done about it until the spring of 1940 when invasion seemed imminent. On the evening of 14 May 1940, Anthony Eden launched an appeal on the wireless:

> We want large numbers of such men who are British subjects, between the ages of fifteen and sixty-five, to come forward now and offer their services . . . The name of the new force which is now to be raised will be Local Defence Volunteers [LDV].

Soon men were rolling up to the police stations in their hundreds, in the Forest as elsewhere, to enrol in the LDV. 'Volunteers will be provided with uniforms and will be armed,' Eden had said. But at first their uniform was just an armband marked LDV and nothing much in the way of weapons. A few shotguns, perhaps a rifle or two and some improvised weapons had to serve a whole platoon. They drilled with broom handles, made 'Molotov Cocktails' (bottles filled with petrol) and prepared barricades.

The remains of some of these preparations can still be seen. At Mitcheldean, until recently, there was an iron ring (to which the roadblock or barricade was fixed) in the rock on the Abenhall road and there are still some remains of a trench at Barton Hill. These were the only barricades at Mitcheldean although there are another five roads leading into Mitcheldean. 'The Germans weren't supposed to come by those roads,' explained a former member of the LDV but he sounded no more convinced by the explanation than I felt.

Another member of the Mitcheldean platoon recalls:

We had a dug-out on a hill just above the railway station. Every Sunday morning, up the Stenders for rifle practice. Two of us were sent up the hill by Bradley Court at 4 every morning to wait for the invasion; one with a rifle and no bullets, the other with no rifle and two bullets.

J.B. remarked that, at Newnham, the main job of the LDV was:

to prevent the Germans from sailing up the river or from landing on the banks. Why the Germans would want to sail up the Severn past Newnham . . . and from where always defeated me, even at that age [schoolboy]. But patrol they did.

At Awre they had some sort of trench down by the river; their job was like Newnham's, and they did man it in earnest once. The message came, via someone who was rather deaf, that the Germans had arrived at Dursley. So as many as could be mustered went down to the lonely trench by the river to await and then repel the enemy as best they could. Legend has it that a few had the presence of mind to gather some crates of bottled beer from the Red Hart en route. Next morning they heard that the Germans had landed in Jersey.

'I think we might ask whoever is responsible for the LDV in the area to see that no rifle is issued to an individual unless the person has control over his faculties,' said the chairman of West Dean CD Committee.

On 23 July 1940 Winston Churchill referred to the LDV as the 'Home Guard' and soon afterwards that became the official name and the armbands marked LDV were replaced by ones marked HG. Proper uniforms and weapons came later.

Ronald Walter Clement Smith was a baker at Drybrook. He was also a Special Constable. At 10 p.m. on 19 August 1940 he was driving home from police duties accompanied by W.G. Robbins, headmaster of Ruardean Hill School, who was also a

Drybrook Home Guard on parade.

Special Constable. Three members of the Home Guard were on duty at the Bailey, Yorkley, and one of them signalled with a red light in order to stop Mr Smith's car. But the car did not stop. It went past the members of the Home Guard, and one of them fired at the rear of the vehicle which then went out of control. The shot had penetrated Mr Smith's back.

Dr W.H. Tandy, who lived at Parkend, was called to the scene. He has recorded the episode in his book *A Doctor in the Forest*.

'What happened?' I asked. 'This chap shot him,' replied the constable (PC Fardon). He went over to the man with the rifle, took it from him and said 'I'll take charge of that'. 'He should have stopped when I flashed my torch,' said the man. I recognized him. He was an elderly man who lived at Oldcroft. He had been in the Boer War and the '14 to '18 war, an old soldier. He was holding a torch in his hand. It was about the size of a packet of twenty cigarettes and had a piece of red paper fixed over the bulb by a rubber band.

Mr Smith was taken to the Bailey Inn where he died almost immediately. The next night Dr Tandy was called to a sick child at Yorkley. Understandably he kept a sharp look-out for any tiny red lights.

On the way back, as I got to the railway level-crossing at Parkend, a hurricane lamp with a red cloth over it was being waved in the middle of the road. I stopped at once. Some figures came towards me. I wound down the car window. 'What's up?' I asked. A bayonet was suddenly thrust through the open window in front of me, and a light flashed on my face. Then a voice said 'Oh! It's only the doctor,' and the bayonet was withdrawn. . . . As I undressed before going to bed that night I noticed that the knot in my tie had been cut by the bayonet. I suddenly went all hot and cold as I realized how near that knot was to my carotid artery.

At the enquiry about the Special Constable's death, the old soldier said, 'I saw this car coming, I flashed my torch. The car did not stop, so I fired'. At the inquest held in September a verdict of 'excusable homicide' was recorded.

A Drybrook man remembers having to guard the reservoir on Ruardean Hill until 2 a.m. – 'There were three of us, but only one rifle'. Why the reservoir had not to be guarded after 2 a.m. was never explained. At Ruardean Hill itself they were 'out every night for weeks', had manoeuvres on Robinswood Hill and every other Sunday at Lydney Park, to which they were taken in Albert Meek's bus. G.L., another Ruardean Hill man, remembers:

In the summer of 1940 the Ruardean Hill platoon mounted nightly two-man patrols on the hill, with orders to pay particular attention to the security of the underground reservoir. At that time its total firing power consisted of one rifle and two rounds of ammunition. One man would carry the rifle and one the bullets. After one hour, halfway through the shift, they would solemnly change over.

Eventually there was enough ammunition to permit a

little target practice in a disused quarry. There was one occasion when a sergeant gave the command 'One round, rapid fire'.

Blank ammunition was never issued so our little exercises assumed a comic aspect. Orders on these occasions were, on encountering an 'enemy', to point the rifle and shout, 'Bang, you're dead'. Such confrontation usually dissolved into laughter and the collapse of the exercise.

On a Sunday morning in the autumn of 1940, we joined with other platoons to engage in our first big exercise, defending the Forest from an attack in the Lydney area. Our platoon didn't last long. At an early stage we were 'killed' or 'captured' and left to ourselves in an orchard.

At the conclusion of the exercise, as we were making our way back to our buses, we were told that the General who had assessed our exercise wanted to see us march past him. Somewhat disgruntled we formed up. Our uniforms consisted of khaki denim overalls. The rag-tag army passed before him, rifles at all angles on our left shoulders, our right arms which should have been swinging in unison, were clutched around our middles, desperately trying to hold in the apples which filled our denim blouses to overflowing.

Westbury Home Guard had parades on Sunday mornings and Wednesday evenings and could afterwards be seen marshalled outside the Red Lion, waiting for opening time. I rather think Home Guard parades helped to create a beer shortage. If men had not been drawn into the villages most of them would have been busy in their gardens and not bothered to visit the pubs.

In one exercise Westbury had to try to invade Longhope. The platoon rode towards Longhope in the Westbury cattle haulier's lorry. On the outskirts of Longhope the local haulier was stopped and challenged.

'What have you got in that lorry?'

'Just livestock.'

'Right, pass.'

And that's how Westbury took Longhope.

Officers of the Forest of Dean Home Guard, including members from Longhope, Mitcheldean and Westbury.

S.H. of Drybrook remembers, 'Any time when Hubert and I were coming back at night we'd stop anyone and ask for identity cards.'

W.D. remembers:

Every district had an Invasion Committee and a War Book – the plan was to destroy everything that could be of use to the enemy. St Briavels had one Ross rifle (Canadian issue) and a few shotguns. At Brockweir, one member of the Home Guard, a clergyman, called halt to a man and asked him his business and the man threatened to throw him into the river. The Brockweir Home Guard had its HQ at the old school by the Moravian Church, with duties two nights per week and occasional church parades. The Home Guard was often in charge of the weekly dances at the MacKenzie Hall when their wives provided the refreshments. ['I'll never know how they got the ingredients,' said Mrs R.]

Woolaston platoon had two parades in the week and one on Sundays. E.B. has these memories:

There was a small signals office at Lydney. Oh, yes, an officer had an old Hillman car with cable brakes, they piled in with equipment, he reverses and shoots into the front door of the Swan. The Home Guard was backed-up by Great War Veterans. There was an invasion scare, '43 I think, and a full-scale stand-to and we were issued with three rounds of ammo each. We went for tea, came back, had some beer and went home.

Someone else remembers that, 'When the Home Guard came to Popes Hill for exercises we locals were told to stay indoors until they were gone.'

The following extracts give details of some of the duties of Coleford Home Guard during 1942:

COLEFORD HOME GUARD   No. 1 Platoon

Parades

Sunday	Jan	4	General Parade	10.15 a.m.
Monday	"	5	MG Class	7.30 p.m.
Tuesday	"	6	General Parade	7.30 p.m.
Wednesday	"	7	Signals	7.30 p.m.
Thursday	"	8	General Parade	7.30 p.m.

June   Col Marriott of Brockweir reached age limit and retired from command of 4 Glos (Forest Battalion of the Home Guard and was succeeded by Major Leslie Allan (Mitcheldean) who was promoted to the rank of Lieut. Col.

July   Many men had been compulsorily enrolled in the Home Guard recently. There were accusations of apathy or indifference which brought the following retort:

Far too much snobbery, red tape and lack of common sense are displayed by some of those who assume authority in the Home Guard and the Foresters, especially the miners, have a

17 Battalion, Coleford Platoon, 1943. Back row, left to right: J. Evans, V. Hyatt, W. Lane, D. Oliver, E. Rogers, P. Jones, F. Perkins, L. Barter. Front row: W. Cuff, W. Dunn, A. Munday, A. Marshall, N. Adams, W. Morgan.

very strong objection to being barked at by someone whose experience they question and who has had a very much easier job all day than the miners. . . .

We seemed to have reached a stage where everybody who has some authority suffers with a swollen head or some similar disease, and wants to 'boss' their fellows. Will they never learn that to obtain a ready response 'bossdom' must be left out and men treated like human beings.

A Forester

One of my informants said 'A lot of it was necessary but some of the officers and sergeants were enjoying it and kept us at it although we had jobs all day. Oh yes, they were having the time of their lives. It was great fun for them.'

Another informant, speaking of a platoon which shall remain nameless, said:

The Company Sergeant Major was the only one who knew anything of the army, having been in the first war. An excellent man and an excellent soldier. There was one man who had pretensions to greatness, but with little substance and of whom I am reminded by Captain Mainwaring in 'Dad's Army', together with a tall, heavily built grossly overweight man who were the officers.

By September a Home Guard training ground had been established at Longhope Manor: 'by the initiative of O/C 4 Glos (Forest) Battalion of the Home Guard, Lt. Col. G.W. Leslie Allan, the Manor had been converted into a Weekend Battalion School of Instruction'. There were classes in musketry, fieldcraft and camouflage, Sten gun and spigot mortar, grenades and battle procedure.

In October the Home Guard took part in a large-scale exercise at Cinderford. Dr Tandy, who became the Medical Officer, said that 'the Forest of Dean Home Guard became an efficient, disciplined, well-armed body of men – tough miners'.

Cinderford Home Guard.

But not everyone was enthusiastic about attending the constant exercises and parades. In November 1942 a Lydney man was charged with failure to attend Home Guard parades; it was said he had only attended four out of a possible eighty. The accused said he was always on call at Norchard Colliery in case of accidents. Faced with a fine of £12, he said he would accept the alternative of a month's imprisonment. This was the first case of its kind to be heard in Forest courts, but more were to come.

A Joys Green man was fined £4 and 35s. costs on three charges of failure to attend Home Guard parades (maximum fine £30) in the same month. Two months later several Home Guard absentees were fined £1 each at Littledean and there were more cases the following week.

Similar cases continued to happen the following year. One man, absent from parades on eight occasions, was fined £7, and an Oldcroft man, a collier at Princess Royal, who had attended only one out of thirty-five parades, chose to go to prison.

In December 1942 three hundred people went to the Miners' Welfare Hall at Cinderford to hear the band of 4 Glos (Forest)

17 Glos (Wye Valley) Battalion, 1943. Front row: (third left) Major C.C. Street, (fifth left) Lt Col R.G.M. Street, (sixth left) Vice Admiral A.F.B. Carpenter VC RW (Retd).

Battalion which was in splendid form. That same month an officer and an NCO were injured by a bomb in an accident which occurred during a Home Guard demonstration at Tump Quarry, English Bicknor, one Sunday morning. Sergeant Piggott of South Wales was taken to the Dilke Hospital and his right hand had to be taken off at the forearm. Major Street of St Briavels, 17 Glos (Wye Valley) Battalion sustained injuries to an eye, an ear and his face and was taken to Newport Hospital.

The third anniversary of the Home Guard took place in May 1943, and on Sunday 16 May several demonstrations took place to mark the occasion. 'B' Coy, Lydney, at Redhill staged a tactical demonstration of a platoon in attack, of firing a spigot mortar and EY rifles, and held a company parade through Lydney with the battalion band in attendance. At Bathurst Park there was a display of arms and equipment. 'A' Coy (Forest) held demonstrations and a march past at Parkend and similar demonstrations were held at Coleford.

On 1 November 1944 the Home Guard was stood down but not disbanded, and the 4th and 17th Battalions held their final parades.

CHAPTER EIGHT

WAITING FOR THE ENEMY

Last week the Forest buzzed with rumours of spies, parachutists and casualties. They were all unfounded.

Forest Newspapers

Lord Haw Haw says Blakeney clock is slow.

Lord Haw Haw says people in the Forest of Dean are reduced to eating acorns.

Rumours like these were rife during the war years. Many were instigated by Lord Haw Haw, the chief German broadcaster in English. (According to people who had always been told by someone else, Haw Haw was given to remarking about clocks all over the country.) Haw Haw's real name was William Joyce, a Fascist who had fled to Germany in 1939. His nickname arose from his supposedly aristocratic tone of voice. Possibly the Government was more rattled by him than the public were because it issued a warning against listening to him. For several years, the Government seemed to fuel rumours that there would be an invasion. In the spring of 1942 a Ministry of Information speaker at the Miners' Welfare Hall, Cinderford, told his audience, 'Don't think "If there is an invasion" but "When there is an invasion" and get ready to deal with it'.

It was a time for rumours – 'I met a man who told me . . .". Spies were a favourite topic. It was said there was a spy at Gatcombe and more at Blaisdon Hall. Rumour had it that some of the Irish priests there were spies. They would flash signals to German aircraft at night. That was why the bombs fell round Blaisdon – the Germans were trying to bomb the

What do I do...

if I come across German or Italian broadcasts when tuning my wireless?

I say to myself: "Now this blighter wants me to listen to him. Am I going to do what he wants?". I remember that German lies over the air are like parachute troops dropping on Britain — they are all part of the plan to get us down — *which they won't.* I remember nobody can trust a word the Haw-Haws say. So, just to make them waste their time, I switch 'em off or tune 'em out!

Cut this out — and keep it!

Issued by the Ministry of Information
Space presented to the Nation by The Brewers' Society

What do I do...

if I hear news that Germans are trying to land, or have landed?

I remember that this is the moment to act like a soldier. I do *not* get panicky. I *stay put.* I say to myself: Our chaps will deal with them. I do *not* say: "I must get out of here." I remember that fighting men must have clear roads. I do *not* go on to the road on bicycle, in car or on foot. Whether I am at work or at home, I just *stay put.*

Cut this out—and keep it!

Issued by The Ministry of Information.
Space presented to the Nation by The Brewers' Society.

The Ministry of Information bombarded the public with many pieces of advice, some more useful than others.

Hereford–Gloucester railway line because trains were carrying explosives to or from Hereford. Perhaps some trains did carry explosives, but otherwise the rumours were quite untrue and completely absurd. No doubt there were many similar tales about other parts of the Forest.

There was a malicious rumour in Newnham that a certain well-known and popular inhabitant was signalling to German aircraft as they crossed the Severn. John Billings writes:

Such a ridiculous thing really. Firstly no German plane required to know where it was and secondly he had fought in the First World War and was severely wounded and left for dead on the battlefield. This rumour became so entrenched and worrying that the vicar made reference to it from the pulpit (I was in the choir) in no uncertain terms . . . that if he knew of any person spreading such information, he would go to the police etc. . . .

In 1940 it became a punishable offence (with £50 fine) to pass on any rumour likely to cause 'alarm and despondency'. A campaign against giving secrets inadvertently to the enemy produced such slogans as 'Careless Talk Costs Lives', 'Walls Have Ears', and 'Be Like Dad Keep Mum'.

On 31 May 1940, with the threat of imminent invasion, an order was made for taking down 'any sign which furnished any indication of the name of, the direction of, or the distance of any place'. Signs and often their posts as well were removed, milestones were defaced. Fortunately we never learned how much this would hinder invaders, but it certainly made things difficult for many inhabitants of Britain. With the blackout and the removal of the names of railway stations it made travelling very difficult. Three years later villages were allowed to identify themselves again.

At the same time the ringing of church bells was banned, except in the advent of invasion when they would be used to sound the alarm. In July the Government announced, 'the duty of the public in the event of invasion is to remain where they are unless instructed to leave'. In November 1942 the *Dean Forest Mercury* reported that the bells of Newnham Church were heard again after a silence of over two years. Two short peals were rung in the morning prior to the service. Newnham was not alone in this case, when church bells were rung as a thanksgiving after the El Alamein victory. The ban was lifted in 1943.

In June 1940 the War Office issued some instructions for the LDV who were 'neither trained nor equipped to offer strong prolonged resistance . . . they will therefore best fulfil their role by observation. . . .' The LDV were also expected to guide

Officers of Cinderford Home Guard.

regular troops, serve as sentries, and look out for spies, parachutists and strangers. They set up barricades; at Huntley they pushed a large tree trunk across the road. At Dunkley's Corner and at Elton there were roadblocks too, and men stood at crossroads with an odd assortment of weapons. Fortunately these puny roadblocks, and weapons, were never put to the test.

Cinderford Home Guard manned look-out posts at Speech House, Edge End, and Heywood. As we've already seen the Home Guard were assiduous in stopping travellers. The Cinderford unit once stopped a hearse coming from Westbury Infirmary and demanded to look inside the coffin.

There are tales of parachutists disguised as nuns. Dr Tandy tells the story of a clergyman being marched to Lydney Police Station with a gun in his back. His captors informed the station sergeant, 'They're coming down in Holland dressed like this'.

While haymaking a farmworker fancied he saw a parachutist – or was it parachutists? – land on Nottwood Hill, Blaisdon.

Members of the Royal Artillery from the Jordan Hill Searchlight turned out in pursuit and so did what members of the Westbury Home Guard were available. It caused some excitement, but not as much as you might expect. Unless memory plays me false, most people took things calmly, as a matter of course. Come to think about it, this was about the only thing to do. Perhaps we were all expecting the worst and each day was a bonus when it didn't happen. The parachutist or parachutists on Nottwood Hill, despite a diligent search, were never found and we were none the worse for that. I happened to observe the farmworker being interviewed by the Royal Artillery officers and Westbury Home Guard officers – he did not look happy. Later we learned that the farmworker might have mistaken those whirlwinds that take hay up in a spiral for parachutes. A less charitable explanation was that he had drunk too much cider.

In order to make the landing of enemy aircraft difficult, farmers were instructed to build their haystacks in the centre of fields and to leave wagons and implements dotted about in fields. Whatever farmers and everybody else lacked in those days they never lacked orders and advice. A 'Medical Officer' wrote an article in the *Forest Newspapers* suggesting that, 'If the sirens disturb your sleep lettuce can help you'.

Other people also thought the Germans had arrived, as one Forest resident explained:

My husband and a neighbour, both of whom were Specials, had to guard the Severn Bridge one night. They thought we, their wives and children, would be safer in the old salmon house down by the river. A silly idea, but we didn't think so at the time. We went down there and some time later we were disturbed by the sound of aeroplanes. That's the Germans again we thought. Then we heard another sound – coming towards us – the sound got louder. It's the Germans, they're here and they're marching towards us. We were terrified but we did venture a peep out through the window and saw by moonlight – horses. They must have been disturbed by the planes. We never spent another night down there.

To hinder any invasion forces, cars were required to be immobilized if they were left unattended.

More regulations were issued in that summer of 1940. It became an offence to leave a car unattended without first immobilizing it – removing the ignition key and locking all doors and windows. But locked doors were no deterrent with open-top cars. And to a wily parachutist – and surely all parachutists would be wily – the absence of an ignition key would present little difficulty. So a part of the engine had to be removed, usually the rotor arm. Doctors and roundsmen were excused this last requirement provided they observed the others and were not absent for more than five minutes.

If the police suspected a car was not immobilized they could take 'reasonable steps', such as deflating the tyres. A Westbury man – and a Special Constable at that – left his car unattended at Minsterworth without removing the ignition key. At the first case of its kind to be heard at Gloucester County Petty Sessions he was fined 10s. It must have given the wardens at Sedbury, and possibly elsewhere, some quiet satisfaction when the Lydney District Surveyor was fined £1 for failure to immobilize his car – although the ignition key was removed and the doors were locked, the rotor arm had not been removed.

CHAPTER NINE

THE WAR AG

The Emergency Powers (Defence) Act gave the Minister of Agriculture far-reaching powers in order to increase home food production. Most of these powers were delegated to the County War Agriculture Executive Committees (commonly known as War Ags) set up shortly before the war. Soon there were sub-committees, district committees and officials galore. Farms, in effect farmers, were graded into categories A, B and C. As long as they did as they were told, A and B farmers were not worried much by the War Ag; C farmers were helped, chivvied or bullied. One of the functions of the War Ag was to give farmers help if they needed it but some of the district people were neither helpful nor reasonable. Not a lot perhaps but enough acted in a dictatorial manner to tarnish the reputation of others who were reasonable men intent on being helpful. Men who had been unsuccessful as farmers themselves often turned up on farms as War Ag officials to give advice and orders, to the scorn of the working farmers who called them 'broken-down farmers'.

The War Ags virtually controlled farmers; a farmer was compelled to do as he was told. If he did not, or if the War Ag considered his farm not up to standard, then the War Ag could dispossess him of his farm, which included turning him and his family out of the farmhouse as well. The farmer had no right of appeal, except to the War Ag, the very organization which was dispossessing him.

However, without the War Ags the increase in food production would not have been achieved. And this involved a change in farming with the emphasis on arable production and on an increase in milk. Every farmer with over thirty acres was given a quota of land to plough, which was increased from time to time. He was ordered to grow corn – especially wheat – sugar-beet and potatoes. Some farmers in the Forest district had never grown these crops before. Local farmers grumbled, in particular about growing sugar beet or potatoes – both in those days were very tedious and laborious crops to produce. They grumbled too about the 'broken-down farmers' who had 'landed cushy jobs'. Sometimes they had just cause to grumble. At the beginning of the war it had been said that the mistake of trying to grow crops, such as wheat, on unsuitable ground, as had been made during the First World War, would not be repeated. It was repeated.

Some farmers didn't own the necessary machinery, not even a horse plough, and only a very few had a tractor. It was to be two or three years before many farmers owned tractors, which could only be obtained if the War Ag granted a permit. The few contractors who did own tractors and ploughs were kept busy. 'Plough by day and night' said the Ministry. One Westbury man did just that, snatching a few hours' sleep under a hedge when darkness fell and resuming ploughing when the moon rose.

Farmers were encouraged to plough at all hours.

The War Ags had tractors, machinery (they had a depot at the fruit market in Westbury parish) and men. The War Ags' charges for threshing (per day) were:

Threshing machines and two men	£4 10s.
Threshing machine, wire baler and three men	£8 10s.
Board money per man	5s.

Prices were controlled, machinery and labour were scarce. Because most pig and poultry food had been imported there was a great reduction in the pig and poultry population – the latter leading to a serious egg shortage. Rabbits and wireworms were plentiful though, and both were harmful to arable crops. The vice-chairman of the Gloucestershire War Ag said rabbits were now worth money and 'everybody was after them'. Unfortunately not many were catching them. And despite the shortage of meat and all the men the War Ag employed as rabbit catchers, rabbits remained plentiful and devoured growing crops. Wireworms in ploughed-up pasture lands devoured potatoes and the roots of corn, pigeons devoured ripening wheat in the fields and rats devoured it in the stack.

Coupons were issued for a limited amount of dairy, pig and poultry food, and permits had to be obtained in order to buy barbed wire or binder twine. It was illegal to use binder twine for straw trussing or any other purposes, except tying sheaves and for thatching, after the Control of Binder Twine Order 1944. Wire netting had to be erected round stacks being threshed. A War Ag official might come at any moment to see if this rule was being observed. Rats jumped over the wire, men tripped over it and swore. After threshing or at any other time it was an offence to have an undeclared sack of corn on the premises.

The blackout made farmwork at both ends of the day very difficult in the winter and Double Summer Time was cursed throughout the summer. A Westbury farmer of the old school refused to observe what he called 'war time' and got in a terrible muddle.

All kinds of people came to 'lend a hand on the land', land

War Ag officials and land girls greeted Queen Mary when she visited the WLA camp on War Ag land at Minsterworth.

girls (official and unofficial), Irishmen, British soldiers, townspeople, Italian and German prisoners of war. Once we had several land girls helping with threshing. Jack, the driver of the threshing machine, was just giving the girls some cider when their supervisor arrived. She was a large, formidable woman. 'Won't that stuff harm my gels,' she said. It was not a question. 'Why, ma'am,' replied Jack, wide-eyed, his face red with cider and black with oil, and looking as innocent as he could, 'it'll do 'em the world o' good.' 'Huh!' she snorted. 'Well just don't give them any more.'

Here and there the War Ag took over land and farmed it, not always successfully. At one farm in Longhope they built a stack of oats on top of a hill and then found they could not get the machine up there to thresh it. At another they grew nothing but potatoes one year and left the clamps inadequately protected against frost so that the whole crop turned rotten. On one farm the corn stacks at both top and bottom were inadequately protected, rain seeped in from the top, damp from the bottom, and the middles were destroyed by rats. And by attempting to cultivate at the top of May Hill a lot of much needed machinery was badly damaged. And yet they took an 86-year-old farmer to court because he had not ploughed a wet corner in one of the fields which he had been ordered to plough-up. In evidence the contractor said his tractor would have been bogged down had he attempted it. On examination the War Ag official admitted that the rest of the farm was well cultivated and that both crops and stock were good.

In October 1944 Foot and Mouth disease broke out at Yorkley – it was thought to be the first outbreak in the Forest since the First World War. The Chief Veterinary Officer of the Ministry of Agriculture came and made his headquarters at the Feathers Hotel, Lydney, from where he directed the work of a number of Ministry Inspectors and the police. Despite this the disease spread through the Forest; first pigs were infected and then sheep and cattle. Well over three hundred animals were slaughtered in

Harvesting with a binder pulled by a Standard Ford tractor.

The Women's Land Army recruited over eighteen thousand women, who carried out a wide variety of agricultural work. Most were employed by the War Ag itself.

West Dean and then over one hundred animals in East Dean following outbreaks at Ruspidge, Crump Meadow, Crabtree and Littledean. Another outbreak then occurred at English Bicknor. The authorities ordered the rounding up and enclosure of all sheep, cattle, pigs and goats that had been running in the Forest. By then the number of animals slaughtered was estimated to be in thousands.

At its meeting in March 1945 Westbury Branch of the National Farmers Union voted against the continuation of the War Ag. The Agricultural Executive Committees (dropping 'War' from their name) continued for some years after the war had ended.

CHAPTER TEN

WOMEN'S LAND ARMY

A Women's Land Army (WLA) was formed in 1917; eighteen thousand women were enrolled and they undertook all kinds of agricultural work. In May 1939 the Minister of Agriculture appointed a WLA Committee and at the outbreak of war a second WLA came into being. The WLA organization recruited, trained and placed land girls in employment, and was responsible for their welfare, accommodation and provision of their uniform.

The WLA uniform consisted of a green jersey, brown corduroy breeches, thick stockings, a wide-brimmed brown hat and brown overcoat, fawn shirt and green tie, but for much of the work they did they wore brown overalls. Their pay, fixed by the Ministry in 1939, was 28s. for a forty-eight hour week, but was later increased, with seven days' leave per year.

The land girls were employed in agricultural, horticultural or forestry work. Girls who had a regular job on a particular farm were billeted in the farmhouse or near the farm. A lot of girls lived in hostels – there was one between Newnham and Blakeney.

Most were employed by the War Ag and usually worked in gangs on farms. Some spent a lot of the year threshing – one of the dirtiest and hardest jobs on the farm – how they stuck it was a wonder. Others spent their time catching rats, another unpleasant job. But as far as I know there were no medals for land girls. Those in forestry were part of the Timber Corps, usually measuring timber or working in sawmills. A number of girls in the Forest, not belonging to the WLA, also did forestry work; several were employed at the Nagshead Nursery at Parkend. At Parkend, the building which had housed the first School of Forestry was turned into a hostel for the WLA.

WLA and WTC girls, with the Matron, outside the Forestry School hostel at Parkend.

One former land girl remembers:

I'd been given some training at the Land Army school, how
to milk cows, clean milk production and all that. I got a bit
of a shock when I started on a farm [in the Forest district],
the cowshed was dirty, the utensils weren't very clean and
the cows were dirty. At my first milking I asked for some
water and a cloth to clean the cows' udders. That gave them
a shock. One of them went away but I could hear him
saying to the farmer, 'That girl you've bin an' got's askin' for
water an' all manner, 'er wants to wash the cows, an' this is
only the start.' 'Oh dear,' I heard the farmer say, 'I knowed it
was a mistake to have a female about the farm.'

Connie Betterton has recorded her memories as a member of
the Women's Timber Corps, working in the Forest of Dean. She
had never heard of the Forest of Dean until she was posted to
Cinderford in 1943 with one other girl. At first they were taken
to work by lorry but were later given bicycles. As a town girl

Forestry girls at Nagshead Nursery. Mrs Harris (front row, second left) had just heard that her husband was in a Japanese prisoner of war camp.

from Yorkshire her main difficulties were learning to identify trees, understanding the Forest dialect and making Foresters understand her:

> The Head Forester was Frank Watson, who was very kind and tolerant of our mistakes. His daughter Megan was a member of the WTC and for a time I worked with her at the Cannop Sawmill. . . .
>
> At different times we worked for Foresters Percy Daniels and Harry Davies, sometimes cycling, sometimes being taken by lorry, but always having to get up at crack of dawn. . . . Besides measuring for the local men, we also worked with the 129 Company of Royal Engineers who felled a lot of timber at Green Bottom woods, Littledean. Also working in those woods were Italian POWs. I remember them, not for their hard work, but for their happy attitude. . . .

Apart from measuring logs, counting pit props, measuring cordwood, time had to be spent in the 'office', a wooden hut, working out piece-work rates, wages and filling in returns. . . .

Land girls wages had increased since 1939, but only slightly. Connie Betterton remembers:

Money was a constant problem. After we had paid for our board and lodging we were left with about £1 a week. . . . Visits home every holiday [Bank Holidays] were a must; so four visits a year had to be budgeted for. At first we were allowed only one free travel warrant a year. Later this was increased to two. . . .

In 1941 Juliette de Bairacli Levy was a member of the WTC and working in the Forest of Dean. When she found her work kept her imprisoned in the sawmills among shrieking machines she objected and started as a labourer, land-clearing and tree-

Forestry girls at Nagshead Nursery.

planting. She remembers, 'Throughout the working hours in the Forest there was an unceasing orchestra of birds, especially the sweet fluting of blackbirds and thrushes, and the merry bell-ringing of the tits.'

In June 1940 about twenty members of the WLA in the Forest helped to quell an outbreak of fire over two or three acres of woodland. The fire flared up fiercely and about sixty people, including the land girls and Crown woodmen, fought the fire which was checked at a belt of chestnut trees. The area where the fire had occurred had been cleared for pitprop timber and the only damage was the destruction of some cordwood. Another fire occurred at Staple End in July and about one hundred and fifty workers fought it.

By August 1943 the WLA had reached its peak strength with eighty thousand members; the county of Gloucestershire employed the fourth largest number. The WLA continued to operate for several years after the war had ended and was not disbanded until 30 November 1950.

Land girls in their working clothes pause to smile for the camera during a busy day in the fields.

CHAPTER ELEVEN

DIG FOR VICTORY

The Dig for Victory campaign began at the outbreak of war. The Ministry of Agriculture seemed to distribute its leaflets recklessly; in 1942 alone ten million were issued. The public was bombarded by Government propaganda, which included advertisements in the press and on hoardings.

Perhaps the propaganda paid off because everywhere there was an enthusiasm for growing vegetables and allotments were in demand. Coleford was commended for the good work on its allotments and Aylburton's were described as 'model allotments'. In fact Aylburton made quite a name for growing large vegetables, although it did have rivals.

It seems that 1941 was a wonderful year for large vegetables. The following list gives details about just some of the bumper harvest:

Eighty-three potatoes of usable size were grown on one root in a Longhope garden.

A mushroom grown at Aylburton measured $13\frac{1}{2}$ inches across, $34\frac{1}{2}$ inches circumference and weighed $1\frac{1}{2}$ lb. Also at Aylburton, a cucumber 2 ft long and weighing $2\frac{1}{2}$ lb was grown at the Globe Inn.

A tomato grown in the open air at Bream weighed 11 oz. An open-air plant at Mitcheldean produced a tomato weighing 12 oz, and one truss with thirty-seven tomatoes which weighed 5 lb 6 oz. From a shilling packet of seeds, 1,363 lb of tomatoes, one weighing 14 oz, were grown at Westbury Institute. Not to be beaten Aylburton produced a tomato that weighed $12\frac{1}{2}$ oz, and a sunflower $15\frac{3}{4}$ inches wide on a plant $17\frac{1}{2}$ ft tall.

Many people responded to the call to grow their own vegetables.

Five carrots weighing 10 lb were grown at Highfield, Lydney, and a turnip weighing 15 lb 10 oz was grown at Owen Farm, Coleford.

In 1942 a heavy plum crop was produced but not so many large vegetables, but in 1943:

Mr Fred Ward on Ruardean Hill grew a tomato which weighed 1 lb and Mr Rowland Beddis of Ruspidge grew a cucumber weighing 3 lb 4 oz. At Milkwall Mr W. Deane moved some earth in his garden and found a self-set potato with haulm 6 ft 9 inches high. The root had forty-three potatoes with a total weight of 21 lb, including three weighing 17 oz each and two weighing 1 lb 5 oz each.

The allotments were scenes of much activity. John Billings recalled:

Daily, people would advance towards them with their spades, forks, rakes, hoes, over their shoulders like rifles. This ritual had several benefits: it got the men out of the house and away from their wives; it could always be substantiated that it was important growing food, saving money, exercise, war effort and all that; and lastly it raised a thirst which could be satisfied at The Club, Lower George, The Railway, Upper George, the Ship. . . . One day the baker was walking around the allotments chatting here and there, when he came upon a large patch of strawberries. He complimented the grower, adding 'they fairly made my mouth water'. Turning slowly the owner said, looking about him, 'Well there's room to spit here'.

At the Government's request Women's Institutes started Preservation Centres to prevent fruit going to waste. The Government provided the sugar, which was useful as housewives had little sugar to spare from their rations for jam-making. It also provided most of the equipment – the WIs of the USA sent a present of canning machines – and paid for some of the fruit. Members who made the jam were not allowed to buy the jam; it had to be sold as part of the jam ration. Not many villages in the Forest had electricity so some jam had to be boiled on oil stoves, and everybody hated the wasps which gathered round. In the Forest there were criticisms of the 'Jam Scheme'. However, there was praise for the members of the Fruit Preservation Centres in West Dean.

At a WI Group Rally held at Whitecroft in 1942, institutes were asked to collect herbs, foxgloves in particular. Aylburton and Bream WIs had already started. At Bilson the members were asked to gather more herbs, especially foxgloves and nettles. By August the gathering of herbs in the Forest was in full swing, Boy Scouts helping with the herb harvest. The nettle season started in May and continued until the end of September; the foxgloves had been gathered in July. Fortunately, foxgloves were in abundance in the Forest, flourishing in the open spaces created in the woodlands by the large amount of timber felling that had gone on since the beginning of the war.

Jam Making and Fruit Bottling

There is still a great shortage of food throughout Europe, and it is vital that everyone should help by growing all they can in gardens and allotments and preserving for winter use.

Home-made jams—"the sort that Mother makes"—and home-grown bottled fruits are the real thing : a source of pride to the housewife and of enjoyment to the family.

Preserve all you can : do not let any fruit be wasted. You will help yourself and help hungry Europe.

The WI's Preservation Centres helped to use up fruit, which would otherwise have gone to waste, in jam making and preserving.

Other herbs were in demand for medicines, including coltsfoot and deadly nightshade. After gathering, these plants had to be dried before being sent away. Drying trays were made from cheesecloth or old net curtains tacked on to old boxes.

The Hedgerow Harvest was another task undertaken by the WIs and the WVS, with help from the children. This harvest included elderberries, blackberries, rowan-berries, sloes, crab apples and hips. The Ministry of Health had announced that hips were twenty times as rich in Vitamin C as oranges and appealed for a national rose hip collection. Children were paid 3*d*. for each pound of hips they collected.

CHAPTER TWELVE

SAVE FOR VICTORY

The scrap metal drive was launched in January 1940. I suppose the cannon that stood outside the Red Lion at Westbury and the one at the Cliff at Newnham disappeared during this campaign. A lot of railings disappeared too, although why some did and others didn't is a mystery. The first reference I have found to the confiscation of iron railings in the Forest is from September 1941:

West Dean RDC
Requisition of Unnecessary Railings
Notice is given that on or before 1 November 1941 the work of removal will commence with the railings in the following places:

Parishes of Coleford, English Bicknor, Lydbrook, Newland, Staunton and West Dean.

It is hoped that the owners will be prepared to make a free gift of their railings etc. to the nation, but property owners who desire to claim compensation may obtain the appropriate form from the undersigned.

H.A. Jones
Clerk to WD RDC

In September the Lydney Surveyor reported that Lydney's salvage effort was disappointing and the district could do better. In October, however, he was pleased with the good response to the salvage drive. In January 1942 he was again disappointed over the Lydney Rural District's salvage results. But by May he was reporting better results once more. Meanwhile there was trouble at the West Dean Council where members were at loggerheads over the confiscation of railings. A resolution that the council should refuse to comply with the instruction from the Ministry of Works was eventually dropped.

Householders were implored all the time to put things aside for salvage, including pots and pans. How the donors managed when bereft of pots and pans was not explained. One suspects they went out and bought new ones if they could find them. And I, for one, suspect the frugal housewives of the Forest of Dean had better sense.

The WVS as usual was at the forefront of the campaign to save metal, wool, paper and so on. 'Use as little paper as possible' was a popular maxim. As always the Government gave directions and advice but when it came to wasting paper it knew no bounds. Apart from all the forms, questionnaires, directives and heaven knows what else there was the constant torrent of propaganda leaflets, the large posters and the big advertisements in newspapers. In 1943 the Squander Bug appeared on hoardings, in newspapers and in magazines. This horrible, hairy squander bug incited people, especially housewives, to waste money, and naturally this cartoon figure wore a swastika.

The horrible, hairy Squander Bugs appeared in 1943, inciting people to waste money – advice which was obviously to be ignored.

The Ministry of Supply promoted a Books for Salvage Drive in 1943. The 'Book Drive' in West Dean resulted in the collection of 31,234 books which were allocated as follows: to Libraries, 834; to the Forces, 3,053; for salvage, 27,347.

Books, newspapers, iron railings, pots and pans, rags and bones . . . it was all potential salvage material. Once it was collected, however, it could cause problems. Newnham, for example, did not know where to store all its waste paper. Railings and other iron taken for salvage often stood in unsightly heaps for months, sometimes years.

Bones were 'urgently wanted' to make glycerine, explosives or fertilizer. Bones had already been removed from imported meat but as the Forest received a large proportion of home-killed meat it had more bones than the average district. So householders were exhorted to 'put them out regularly for salvage each week'.

The various Savings Weeks, such as 'Wings for Victory Week', greatly encouraged people, and the amount of savings generally increased during these periods. Towns and districts set targets. In 1941 it was 'War Weapons' Week' and the Forest's aim was £150,000. At that time a machine gun cost £200; a Lewis gun £60, a service rifle £8 (these figures are approximate only).

In March 1942 it was 'Warship Week' with a target of £175,000. The Lydney programme included: seven bands, a variety concert, a military concert, a lantern lecture, football matches, dances and processions. And of course everyone turned out for the parades – the Military, Home Guard, ARP, Special Constables, Fire Service, WVS, First-aid, and other organizations. . . . That week Lydney collected £109,015, West Dean £81,289, and East Dean £71,151.

'Wings for Victory Week' took place in May 1943, and 'Salute the Soldier Week' in June 1944. At 6.30 p.m. on Saturday 3 June, Cinderford had a Grand Parade of Naval and Military Services, including US Forces, Home Guard, Forest of Dean Sea Cadets, Air Training Corps, Girls Training Corps, Cinderford Army Cadets, US Band, Cinderford Town Band and Drybrook Band. Among the week's activities was a baseball game between the US Forces' teams.

The 'Wings for Victory' Parade at Newnham (above). 'Wings for Victory' Week was held from 7 to 15 May 1943. The various events listed in the programme (below) helped to increase savings.

Friday, May 7th to Saturday, May 15th

FRIDAY. THE OPENING CEREMONY.
The LOCAL SERVICES will parade at The Victoria at 7-45 p.m., and will march through the streets to the Saluting Base where the Salute will be taken by
THE HIGH SHERIFF OF GLOUCESTERSHIRE
(Sir Evan Gwynne-Evans, Bt.)
and the SELLING CENTRE will be opened.

SATURDAY. DARTS COMPETITION begins.
A 'Knock out' Darts Competition will be held in Local Centres and Finalists will proceed to the Final (see below). Entrance Fee: One Savings Stamp.

MONDAY. VISIT OF THE MOBILE CINEMA.
The Mobile Cinema will visit the Masonic Car Park in Station Road to give an Hour's Programme of Topical Films. Admission Free.
UNLAWATER SOCIAL EVENING at W.I. Hut at 8 p.m.   Light Refreshments.   Admission: 1/6.

TUESDAY. "WINGS" WHIST DRIVE
In the Club Hall, 7-0 p.m.   M.C.: Mr. R. Atkins. Tickets 1/- each.

WEDNESDAY. "WINGS" DANCE in the Club Hall.
M.C.: Mr. Harry Walch.   For details see small bills.

THURSDAY. "WINGS" CONCERT in the Club Hall.
Items by the Girls of Broombank School.   Cabaret. supported by Local Artistes.
A limited number of Seats will be Guaranteed so take your tickets early.

FRIDAY. A "MAKE AND MEND" EXHIBITION
arranged by MISS KERR and W.V.S. Members In Messrs. Blanton's Shop (by kind permission of Messrs. Blanton). Opening at 5 o'clock.

SATURDAY. FINALS of DARTS COMPETITION.
LIVING WHIST arranged by MISS LACE on the Green at 7-0 p.m.

OTHER ATTRACTIONS will be organised in different parts of the town in the evenings.

All the Forest villages had events — mainly whist drives and dances, although a few villages were a bit more enterprising. All these parades and social activities provided welcome relief and entertainment during the dark days of wartime. Thrift provided the excuse for them, but they probably did a more useful service by boosting morale.

CHAPTER THIRTEEN

EMPLOYMENT

In May 1940 the unemployed figures at the Forest Labour Exchanges were:

Cinderford	129
Coleford	96
Lydney	93
Newnham	28

As more and more men were conscripted and war work in industry and on the land increased, jobs could generally be found. On 14 June 1940 a news item stated:

Every man who is able to work is given a job – at coal mining, munition work or other vital war activity. As soon as a man registers as unemployed he is almost automatically transferred to work of some kind. The intention of the Minister of Labour is to see which of the long-term unemployed can be got back to useful work by training rehabilitation.

Coal mining was the principle industry in the Forest. At the height of coal production in the Forest mines, thousands of men were employed. Here, as in other coalfields, this underground army suffered a steady stream of casualties. Nationwide approximately eight hundred miners were killed in the pits and one hundred and twenty thousand injured in British collieries every year during the war years.

The number of miners employed, however, was gradually decreasing and by the time of the Second World War there were

A miner at work in Lightmoor Colliery.

far fewer miners in the Forest, as figures from Lightmoor Colliery show. This colliery closed down in May 1940. It had opened in 1840 and at its peak employed 1,000 men with a daily output of 1,000 tons. At the time of its closure only 172 men were employed and the daily output was just 18 tons.

In September 1940 the Forest pits, as others throughout the country, were desperately in need of more miners as increased coal output was required for the war effort, but there were fewer miners to achieve this because so many had been called up. It was reported that:

> By 1941 coal stocks had become so low that any under-thirties left in the pits were forbidden to leave and the army released thirty-three thousand ex-miners who were forced to return to their old job.

Some of these men were not willing to return to the mines. In December 1941, at Coleford Police Court, a Coleford man pleaded not guilty to failing to comply with a Ministry of Labour directive to return to work at Princess Royal Colliery. This was the first case of its kind in the Forest.

Just as the early 1940s was an obviously turbulent time worldwide, so there were many disputes and much strife within the world of mining throughout this period. There were constant fights about pay – in March 1942 miners were refused a minimum of £4 5s. per week – and about ownership of the mines themselves – in June 1942 it was announced that the state would control coal mines. Local MP Mr Price warned, however, that if the scheme failed the public would demand public ownership of the mines.

The proposed closure of the New Fancy Colliery generated controversy. The miners and their union, and the colliery owners, wanted to keep the colliery open but in 1944 the Regional Authority of the Ministry of Fuel and Power decided to close it and re-employ its 300 men at other Forest pits.

A working party on a portable mill near the New Fancy Colliery.

Disputes such as these continued throughout the war years. The end of the war coincided with the beginning of the decline of the coal industry and twenty years later all coal mines in the Forest had closed. It was the end of an era and Old King Coal's reign in the Forest was over.

Before the war there was very little employment for women in the Forest. One of the few options for girls was to go into domestic service outside the Forest, and a great many did this. The war changed all that, however. As the number of men in the workforce began to decrease, women were called upon to fill their places on farms, in factories, on the transport system. Women from the Forest also played a major role in the many industries relating directly to the war, such as munitions factories and aircraft factories like the ones at Brockworth, near Gloucester.

Special buses took Foresters to the factories at Brockworth. One day there was an air raid at Brockworth just as some Forest workers were about to go home. Mrs Davis, who lived at Causeway Road, Cinderford, was killed. She had boarded the bus a few minutes before a bomb dropped on it.

Edgar Bradley of Lydbrook was also killed in a raid at Brockworth. He was sitting in the back of Edwards' bus on a Saturday afternoon, waiting to go home, when a bomb fell on some open ground behind the bus. He was still sitting in the bus when it went on its journey to Lydbrook. It was only later that it was discovered that Mr Bradley was dead – killed by some shrapnel which had penetrated the bus and then become embedded in his back.

In July 1942 the Divisional Road Surveyor reported that the performance of women who had been employed as roadworkers in the Forest was 'completely satisfactory'. Sixteen, all volunteers, were employed. They had to travel up to twelve miles a day and were expected to do all kinds of work except for pick and shovel. They never complained. But Councillor S.W. Hatton complained 'perhaps they've worked better since a letter was published in the three Forest newspapers'. Apparently Mr Hatton's criticism of the women road workers at a previous West Dean RDC meeting had 'hurt the girls very much'.

In August Mr Hatton was challenged to do one week's work on the road. He replied that yes, he would provided that:

1. the woman he relieved did his work for the same period.
2. the work was done in Lydbrook parish.
3. he could take shelter when it rained and could share the comfort of the fire.

British Acoustic Films, who produced bomb sights, fire direction tables and other precision equipment, came to Mitcheldean in 1940. The company took over part of the Brewery premises, starting with the old bottling house. Maintenance men, electricians and plumbers were the first workers to arrive, and it was believed there may be as many as

The bottling house at Mitcheldean Brewery.

five hundred who would be coming to the area. Just one month later housing for three hundred BAF employees and their families was needed.

The problem of housing was discussed by East Dean RDC in January 1941. Mr T.W. Little said one of the company's directors had told him that the firm would remain at Mitcheldean permanently. Mr Little also said that East Dean Council should send a representative to ask the Ministry for a loan for building houses. The Chairman expressed doubts and added, 'As you've nothing to do, Mr Little, I suggest you visit Bristol and take up the matter personally'.

In late 1939 the Ministry of Supply decided to erect a 'salvage depot' at Lydney on a site by the banks of the canal. It was expected to employ between 150 and 200 men. The depot would be used for dumping damaged war material and was hailed as 'the first new industry for the Forest of Dean'. Hard on its heels came news of another factory for Lydney which would employ 1,000 men.

A factory for the Aero-Nautical and Panel Plywood Co. Ltd, acting for the Ministry of Supply, was erected alongside the Lydney canal. Building started in 1940 and production began in April 1941. The factory produced plywood for aircraft from Canadian birch and home-grown beech. The imported timber came to Avonmouth and was then transported up the Severn and along the canal where it was unloaded by cranes. It was used in the manufacture of Mosquito aeroplanes and for gliders used for the invasion of Europe in 1944. Ninety per cent of aircraft plywood was imported, almost all the rest was made at Lydney.

Watts of Lydney were making 'gas-conversions' for petrol vehicles. The company also had a naval contract for overhauling generators used on landing craft. The generators and engines were American and special equipment had to be installed. As a result of that contract a canteen was installed at the factory. The motor department was kept busy overhauling commercial vehicles. Six-wheeler lorries, dreadfully overloaded with coils of steel, were continually breaking down, usually at Alvington, Highfield or Sparkes Hill, and mechanics were called out to them most nights.

The manufacture of Mosquito aircraft relied upon plywood such as that produced by the factory built by the canal at Lydney.

In 1943 the Forest was told it must awaken to its needs. Industries were needed to succeed coal mining and there must be a united front for the difficult years ahead. Twelve months later it was announced that contact had been established with seven industries offering post-war employment for over 2,000 men and women.

In West Dean a storm erupted over the appointment of a Conscientious Objector as District Milk Officer. 'As one who refuses to help defend his country, Mr Cooper should not have accepted this job behind which he can shelter in safety while others fight for his freedom,' said S.W. Hatton.

'I reply to that,' said Mr Cooper, 'by saying that I will give up this job and all other work before I will sacrifice my religious feelings.'

Later West Dean RDC imposed a ban on the employment of Conscientious Objectors following a motion from West Dean Parish Council which said, 'They (the RDC) should never appoint a person upholding the sentiments of Conscientious

During the war years Watts of Lydney converted vehicles, such as the car shown here, to run on gas.

Objection to any position created directly or indirectly as a result of war.'

Several letters on the rights or wrongs of this decision were published in the *Forest Newspapers*. The controversy rumbled on into September. Councillor Hatton said, 'COs are only cowards', to which Councillor Hawkins replied, 'You have no right to say that, Mr Hatton'. The West Dean Food Control Committee recommended that Mr Cooper should be dismissed on principle by the Ministry.

In October 1940 a Quaker Conscientious Objector living on May Hill and employed as a teacher at Newent attended a tribunal at Bristol. As he was unable to join the Friends' Ambulance Unit, he decided with the consent of the tribunal, to undertake non-combatant duties, preferably in the Royal Army Medical Corps.

CHAPTER FOURTEEN

SOME OF OUR AIRCRAFT

No enemy aircraft came down in the Forest, but several British aeroplanes crashed in the Forest or the rivers. Most of the aircraft that crashed were from training units. Some of the machines were old or were not airworthy. Ground crews were very hard-pressed and did not have time to give sufficient attention to the aircraft, and some of the pilots were very young and were, perhaps, not as skilful as pilots have to be today. A few aircraft even came to grief by trying to fly under the Severn Railway Bridge. In all RAF Training Command lost 25,000 aircrew, almost half as many as the total lost by Bomber Command which had 55,000 casualties. These tragic accidents, the waste of young lives and the loss of so many aircraft brought the war closer than anything else to the Forest of Dean.

The accident reports reprinted on the following pages should serve to give us an impression of the many dangers that the airmen faced.

21 Oct. 1939	Gloucester Gladiator K6145, 263 Sqn, Filton, crashed into the River Severn near the Severn Railway Bridge. The pilot, Sgt Patrick Watson-Parker, was injured.
April 1940	Hawker Hurricane crashed at Boseley, on Westbury/Flaxley border. Pilot Officer Trouncer was injured.
19 June 1940	Bristol Blenheim L1471, 50 Operational Training Unit (OTU), Aston Down, Stroud, crashed into the Severn off Lydney Harbour.
25 Aug. 1940	Bristol Blenheim L6733, Aston Down, crashed at Tidenham Chase. The pilot, Pilot Officer David MacKintosh Moore-Bell, was killed.

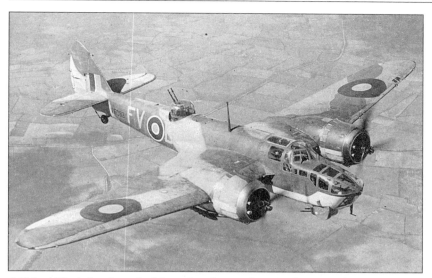

A Bristol Blenheim. Several of these aircraft came down in the Forest during the war.

8 Oct. 1940	Handley Page Hampden 1, 16 OTU 7 Group Bomber Command, Upper Heyford, Oxfordshire, crashed at Home Farm, Highnam. Pilot Officer Albert Frederick Jeffreys (aged 28), Sgt Joseph Edmund Shiels (aged 27), Sgt Richard Thomas Bowtell (aged 22) and Sgt Ralph Alexander Keeling (aged 22) were all killed.
April 1941	Three German airmen, after baling out from their damaged aeroplane near Coleford, surrendered to the first civilians they saw. The prisoners were lodged overnight in Coleford Police Station. The pilot remained in the aeroplane and managed to return to Germany.
29 May 1941	Westland Whirlwind crashed in the Severn at Guscap Rocks, Woolaston.
19 Aug. 1941	Boulton Paul Defiant 74110, 125 Sqn, Charmey Down, crashed at Lower Lydbrook. The pilot,

The Westland Whirlwind that crashed in the Severn at Woolaston, 29 May 1941.

A Boulton Paul Defiant 1 like this crashed at Lower Lydbrook on 19 August 1941.

Sgt Bassow, and Sgt Davis parachuted safely to the ground.

22 Oct. 1941	Hawker Hurricane W9263, 52 OTU, Aston Down, crashed into the Severn near Severn Railway Bridge. The pilot, Sgt A. Cooper (Canadian), survived.
14 Dec. 1941	Westland Whirlwind P7044, 363 Sqn, Filton, crashed at Speech House. The pilot, Sgt Prior, was killed. The force of the impact drove the machine into the ground.
16 Dec. 1941	Hawker Hurricane Z29989, 2 Ferry Pilots Pool, Filton, made a forced landing south-east of Ross. The pilot survived.
23 Jan. 1942	Avro Anson N5324, 6 Air Observers School, 25 Flying Group, Training Command, Staverton, crashed in the Severn at Rodley, Westbury. The purpose of the flight had been a map reading exercise. The aircraft struck high tension cables in very bad visibility. No windscreen wipers were fitted to the aircraft. The pilot, Sgt Philip Pantook (aged 21), Ldg Aircraftsman Robert Palmer (aged 29), Ldg Aircraftsman Reginald Banks (aged 33), and Aircraftsman Herbert Admore (aged 20) were all killed.
8 Feb. 1942	Spitfire R7135, 52 OTU, Aston Down, crashed at Oldbury Sands on the River Severn. The pilot, Sgt J.R. Pierce (Canadian), was killed. His body was washed ashore at Lydney Harbour on 7 April.
24 April 1942	Supermarine Spitfire R7124, 53 OTU, Llandow, Cowbridge, crashed into the Severn at Broadoak, nr Newnham. The pilot, Irishman Sgt Allen Hedley McFall (aged 24), was killed. Eyewitness Mr L. Jackson, of Broadoak, stated that two Spitfires had been 'fooling around' and one of them hit some trees at Elton Corner. It lost

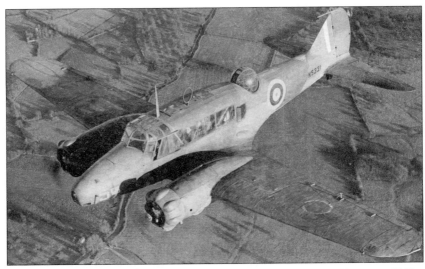

An Avro Anson Mk 1 similar to the one that crashed at Westbury on 23 January 1942 killing all four crew members.

height and then hit the ground, made a hole in the orchard and bounced into the middle of the river. It was a low tide and Mr Jackson waded out to the aircraft, released the pilot and carried him ashore. He was obviously dead as he was cut to ribbons.

2 June 1942   Spitfire N3065, 52 OTU, spun into the ground near Longhope School. The pilot, Sgt D. Cameron (an American serving in the RAF), baled out safely.

7 June 1942   Handley Page Halifax V9977, Telecommunications Flying Unit, Defford, crashed near Welsh Bicknor. Eleven crew and scientists were killed.

28 Jan. 1943   Vickers Armstrong Wellington X3936, 115 Sqn, 3 Group Bomber Command, East Wrentham, Norfolk, crashed into the Wye at Brockweir. Its duty had been minelaying at La Rochelle and the Friesian Islands. The plane was one of six

On 2 June 1942 a Spitfire like these crashed near Longhope School.

aircraft detailed for operations carrying 2 × 1,500 mines. The pilot was unable to locate the target because of an unserviceable compass. The wireless and the Gee navigation aid were also unserviceable and on the return flight the aircraft became lost, travelling 150 miles off course. A searchlight co-operation was unsuccessful, and when the fuel supply became low, the mines were safely jettisoned and the pilot gave orders to abandon the aircraft. The crew baled out as the aircraft was heading towards the river:

Pilot Sgt Plum, unhurt; Sgt N. Newton (Canadian), unhurt; Sgt L. Lane, slightly injured; Pilot Officer G.H. Willis, unhurt; Sgt F. Eaglestone, slightly injured.

Sgt Plum takes up the story:

We jumped out when the fuel had expired, and we landed on the bank of the River Wye, near

Monmouth, and the aircraft itself actually went into the River. Four of the crew were completely unhurt, but Sgt Eaglestone, who was the wireless operator, banged his head at some point in the descent and laid unconscious in a field overnight until he was picked up by the police. . . .

I, myself, landed in the garden of a house and it must have been about two or three o'clock in the morning and raining heavens hard and a filthy night. I banged on the door but nobody wished to make my acquaintance, so I walked towards the river where the aircraft was burning slightly and there I met up with members of the Home Guard who had turned out. They, of course, thought we were Germans.

Norman Plum became a Flight Lieutenant and by 1944 had completed over eighty operations. He was awarded the Distinguished Flying Cross and Bar.

4 May 1944	Percival Proctor Z7217, 4 Reserve Sqn, Madely, Hereford, crashed at Coalway. The crew of two were both killed.
27 Sept. 1944	Hawker Typhoon JP904, 3 Tactical Exercise Unit, Aston Down, crashed 1¼ miles east of Aylburton after a forced landing because of engine failure. The aircraft's duty had been formation practice. Flt Lt R.A. Yates–Earl was unhurt.
7 April 1945	Hawker Typhoon MP127, 55 OTU, Aston Down, crashed at Ashwell Grange Farm, Woolaston. The pilot, Sgt Lattimer, was killed.
6 May 1945	De Havilland Mosquito KB233 crashed by the railway line at Purton Pill (Lydney side). It had been on a night training exercise. Sqn Ldr W.H. Corbett DFC (aged 25) and Lt Per Breivik (aged 29 and of the Royal Norwegian Air Force) were

The crew of the Vickers Armstrong Wellington which crashed in the River Wye at Brockweir, January 1943. P/Sgt Plum is in the centre of the photograph.

both killed. Lt Per Breivik was the last member of the RNAF to die during the Second World War. It was believed the pilot lost control due to anoxia caused by failure of the oxygen supply. The aircraft broke up in the air. John Nichols of Lydney was walking along the railway line when he saw an American soldier on the line who told him he was guarding an aircraft which had crashed. However, he was allowed to continue and eventually saw lots of camouflaged plywood. The sea wall had been damaged and over the wall was one of the aircraft engines. No wreckage had fallen on the line but one of the crew was found on the line.

CHAPTER FIFTEEN

LIGHT NOTES ON DARK DAYS

With war work, ARP, NFS, WVS, Home Guard, ambulance classes, salvage collection and so forth it was a wonder how anyone actually found time for the entertainments that were on offer in the Forest. But various pastimes and activities were available and, perhaps because of the harshness of real life, they were generally popular and well attended by the people.

Everyone listened to the wireless. Most wireless sets were run on batteries and accumulators; batteries like everything else became scarce and accumulators had to be recharged frequently.

The news was gloomy or terrible, but there was *Itma*, possibly the most popular of all the comedies broadcast during the war. It was crazy, but a relief from the horrific craziness being performed in the real world. For its humour it relied upon topical allusions, atrocious puns and a cast of silly characters presided over by Tommy Handley who delivered his lines like machine gun fire. Doors banged and the various characters entered and said their catch-phrases which became part of the national vocabulary.

Among the popular comedy series were *Garrison Theatre*, in which Jack Warner made his name; *Gert and Daisy*, who were his sisters Elsie and Doris Waters; *Hi Gang*, with Bebe Daniels, Ben Lyon and Vic Oliver, three Americans who chose to stay in Britain during the war. Fortunately there seemed to be a lot of good comedians when good comedians were really needed.

On a more serious plane there was *The Brains Trust* an educational programme consisting of a panel with three regular

Lauri Wylie's 'Wireless Puppets' come back to the microphone today at 3.30

Written and devised by Laurie Wylie this performance of *Wireless Puppets* – RADIO TIMES, 1 August 1941 – was produced by Harry S. Pepper. The artists taking part were far from lifeless marionettes and included Leonard Henry, Marjorie Sanford, Frederick Gregory, Dick Francis, Vera Lennox and Clarence Wright. The show's music came from Sam Rogers and his orchestra. The programme was broadcast from Bristol, the BBC's wartime headquarters of variety, religious and schools broadcasting, music and *Children's Hour*

COMMUNITY

WHISTLING

Join in and whistle with Ronald Gourley and the boys this evening at 6.30

Come along and join in whistling with RADIO TIMES, 11 April 1941

The wireless provided a wealth of programmes to suit all tastes.

members who discussed and tried to answer questions sent in by listeners. The philosopher, Dr Joad, used to preface his answers with 'It all depends on what you mean'. The programme started on 1 January 1941 and by 1943 had a regular weekly audience of ten to twelve million listeners. Very few programmes rivalled it in popularity.

In July 1943 Dr Joad came to the Forest and spoke at a meeting held at Bells Grammar School, Coleford, which was organized jointly by Coleford Workers' Educational Association, the WI, the adult school (night school), the youth club and the Forest branch of the National Union of Teachers.

On Sunday afternoons at 2.15 p.m., *In Your Garden*, with Mr Middleton, was broadcast. These gardening talks were popular at a time when vegetable gardening was of paramount importance to many households.

Other programmes included *Priestley's Postscripts* on Sunday evenings, the *Radio Doctor* one morning a week, *Saturday Night Variety, Monday Night at Eight.* . . . It would be difficult to exaggerate the importance or the popularity of the wireless during these years.

The cinemas were also very popular. Most of them were filled to capacity for performances, and often there was a queue waiting outside. In those days there were cinemas at Cinderford, Coleford and Lydney, with smaller ones at Bream, Drybrook and Lydbrook. Often films were shown in village halls or schools. Originally films were only shown on Mondays to Saturdays.

In October 1942 a proposal to apply to Parliament for an order permitting local cinemas to open for charity on Sundays was rejected by West Dean RDC. Finally the authorities relented and allowed cinemas to open on Sundays. There were also propaganda films. The Ministry of Information had a Sound Film Mobile Unit which came to the Forest and showed films in the villages.

Almost every village held a dance every week, either on Fridays or Saturdays. At the bigger dances the music was often provided by Billy Thomas and his Band. Billy Thomas was the son of a Pillowell smallholder and by 1941 was himself engaged in farming at Little Purlieu near Blakeney. He succeeded in

Billy Thomas and his Gloucester Accordion Band.

converting fifty acres of rough land covered in bracken into arable land. By October twenty-five acres were sown with oats and the remainder would be sown with oats or planted with vegetables by the following spring.

In 1943 an ARP dance was held at Lydbrook Memorial Hall with Harry Roy's Tiger Ragamuffins. (Harry Roy's band was one of the foremost bands in England.) Refreshments were provided by the WVS, tickets cost 5s. 6d. and proceeds went to Red Cross Funds. Almost at the end of the war there was a 'Grand Nautical Ball', in aid of the Merchant Navy, held at Lydney Town Hall.

Concerts were another popular entertainment. The Blackout Frivolities were billed as a 'special attraction' at a variety concert held at Cinderford in aid of the Dilke Hospital Nursing Staff's Theatre Appeal.

During the first summer of the war 'Sutton's Jungle Speedway', with chariots, swing boats and fun fair, was at Blakeney. The invitation was to 'Come in and have a really good

A wartime dance at Mitcheldean.

time'. But there was also a warning: 'Please come early owing to the Black-Out.'

'Holiday Weeks' were introduced. As it was impossible for people to go away on holiday, lots of activities and entertainments were planned for a week during the summer. The idea was to keep people at home and keep them amused, as well as providing them with some relief from their usual routines. Lydney & District Hospital held a Holiday Week over the August Bank Holiday period in 1942. Activities included the annual tea and fête at Bathurst Park on Monday 3 August; an exhibition by the boys of the London Nautical Training School; side shows and competitions; a dance at the Grammar School; a hospital ball and cabaret show; and a cricket match.

CHAPTER SIXTEEN

THEY ARE OVER HERE

The GIs started to arrive in Britain in 1942. Foresters are hazy about the date they actually came to the Forest but suddenly they were everywhere. In the towns, the villages, the pubs, driving about in jeeps. . . .

'They wore rubber-soled shoes. When they came some of them couldn't march and some still couldn't when they left.'

'At first we thought they must all be officers, their uniforms were so good – not like the rough old stuff our soldiers had to wear.'

'They had everything; money, food, cigarettes, chewing gum, candy, nylons.'

'They pinched our girls, the girls went crazy over them.'

'They taught the girls to jive.'

'They were arrogant and loud-mouthed.'

'They were lovely fellows, friendly, generous. . . .'

There was a US camp at Clanna and another at Naas, near Lydney. And where Lydney Industrial Estate is now there was an American depot which employed local civilians:

After a while several Lydney people were wearing American clothes, particularly those khaki-green socks which were issued to American troops. Yes, we were pleased to have the Americans. At a time of scarcity they brought abundance to Lydney.

Several thousand Americans came to Wigpool (between Mitcheldean and Drybrook) and lived under canvas:

They started coming one day, jeeps and vehicles, huge tractors, we'd never seen anything like it, gigantic guns and bulldozers and equipment, we never knew there was such stuff. They had to shunt and shunt to get round Drybrook Corner, oh, they did have a job.

Within a few days they were all over the place. In the pubs they'd put their money, cigarettes, matches, chewing gum, on the counter. Some of them got robbed over money – they didn't understand our money and would plonk down a fistful. They were all white Yanks at Wigpool. They didn't mix, not the white and the black – we were shocked at the whites' attitude towards the blacks. They had a landing strip up at Wigpool and a light plane used to come every day. And they used an old iron mine as a cinema. As far as I know there was no trouble, no fighting and despite all those fellows I never heard of any cases of rape.

They were different Americans at Cinderford – I don't think the Wigpool lot had anything to do with them. At Cinderford they had Military Police parading the streets, we didn't have any at Drybrook.

Some of the American troops at Wigpool used to come to Drybrook Methodist Chapel. I got talking to one about singing, and do you know, he'd never heard of Paul Robeson.

We never had any rowdiness in Drybrook from those young men, except once. That was when there was a dance at the Memorial Hall and a white officer went in, leaving his black chauffeur outside. Along came some white Americans and started worrying this black chap. The black chap ran into the hall and in there some white Americans began to attack him. The local men weren't having that, there were several of them home on leave and they set about the Yanks.

Some of the Americans stationed at Wigpool used to go to the Crown at The Hawthorns to bath and the landlady was allowed extra coal for this purpose. One day her husband was accosted in the street at Cinderford by an American. 'Hey,' he said, 'I'm a relation of yours.' It was discovered that the landlady was related to him and that the American's uncle had the Seven Stars at Cinderford.

A Mitcheldean man remembers the Wigpool Americans for the quantities of cigarettes they gave away or sold very cheaply – Lucky Strike, Camels, Chesterfield. He and others also remember the quantities of cider the American troops drank.

When the Americans were stationed at Wigpool, they began levelling the playing fields at Mitcheldean with their huge machines. They did not quite finish because they had orders to leave in a hurry.

The American troops left Wigpool as suddenly or even more suddenly than they came: 'About two o'clock one morning in 1944 we heard the trucks, all night long we heard them driving away.'

Mr Cook was one of the American troops who came to the Forest:

We were at Broadwell first, under canvas. We found Doughboy [what US troops were called in the First World War] signs, Mustard and Lewisite gas from the First World

Live ammunition, poison gas and explosives near Speech House. This photograph was taken just after the Second World War.

War in the woods by Speech House. We were stacking FS Smoke Shells, Mustard, Phosgene and Lewisite gas in the woods. Phosgene was the most deadly – if all that had escaped the people in Cinderford would not have had a chance. If those woods had been bombed . . .

Some of those gas bombs did leak – we were always finding dead sheep – before we had a proper device to test for leaks a young fellow used to walk past the stacks and sniff. He ended up in hospital. Troops were continually patrolling round the Forest in jeeps, British troops used to comb the woods with Alsations which were kept at the Miners' Hall at Cinderford.

We dug pits twelve feet deep and buried the defective gas bombs – I wouldn't advise anybody even now to sit anywhere in the woods where that gas was buried.

We left Broadwell and went to Nissen huts opposite the White Hart at Ruspidge – those huts were cold to sleep in and damp from condensation. I had my first drink of beer in the Bridge pub down at the bottom. The Speech House was for officers only. We weren't allowed to go to Lydbrook or Coleford either because there were coloured troops stationed at both places. They weren't allowed in Cinderford because it was all whites there.

We were handling AC gas bombs and 400–lb aircraft bombs.

I thought the Forest was beautiful and what intrigued us most about England were the very small lorries and railway carriages. The English people were generous to us. The first Christmas we were here a couple invited me for Christmas dinner – they were wonderful people. I regard Cinderford as my hometown in England, it's where I found my wife.

Several Forest girls married Americans. But no American soldier stationed here was allowed to marry without first getting permission from his commanding officer. An application had to be made to his officer three months in advance. Once an application was received a thorough investigation was made of the applicant before permission was granted or withheld. It was a court martial offence to marry without permission.

American Corporal Techician 5th
Grade Ned Cook and his bride June
Jenkins (of Valley Road, Cinderford),
who were married at St John's
Church, Cinderford.

The coloured troops' main tasks were loading and unloading
and stacking ammunition and constructing bases. Dr Tandy has
noted:

Their main task was stacking poison in the Forest. They
stacked hundreds of thousands of tons of it. It took several
years to remove it when the war was over. . . . I often felt
very apprehensive about the possibilities of those stores of
gas being bombed.

Another resident remarked that:

There were high explosives all through the Forest, stored
in Nissen huts and there were barbed wire fences all round
the woods. Most of the explosives were gone before
D-Day.

American Forces took over the Forestry School at
Parkend (previously a WLA hostel) for their headquarters.
Mr and Mrs Minchin think they came in 1943. Parkend
railway station was the main branch line for bringing in the
ammunition. Prior to D-Day, the ammunition was brought
to Parkend by lorry and put on rail for Lydney and beyond.
Coloured troops unloaded and loaded. 'They worked very
quickly and sang as they worked. Between loads they threw
dice. We liked them, they were very polite when they came
to get water to make their coffee.'

One of my informants remembers that at the dances held at
Parkend Memorial Hall:

There were always two MPs at the door. They also had film
shows and on Independence Day they invited all the village
to a meal. They played baseball in our cricket field but they
just couldn't understand cricket.

Mr Wright of Parkend recalls that:

The Americans had a depot and a workshop near the
crossroads at Cannop. They made roads into the woods
where they stored gas and explosives – in the Parkend
district, Cannop, Speech House, a lot of trees near Speech
House died. The explosives were taken out very quickly at
night, just before D-Day. Convoys of lorries came from the
woods to Parkend Station, others went on by road.

The town hall at Coleford was turned into a canteen for
American Forces by the American Red Cross. The following
notice appeared in the *Dean Forest Guardian*:

Two coloured American girls, well-educated and recruited
from the best type are to assist in running the canteen and
will require accommodation – a bedroom and sitting room.
Terms to be arranged between the householder and the
American Red Cross.

The typical GI, as depicted on the
cover of a magazine.

The Bon Marche shop in Cinderford was turned into a
canteen for American Forces and run by the WVS. The
Americans had taken over the Miners' Welfare Hall, St John's
Hall, and the White Hart at Ruspidge. Local people now held
dances at the Rosalind Hall in Dockham Road until the
Government commandeered it and used it as a shirt factory.
After the war the hall was taken to Dursley.

In late 1944 a Lydney girl, aged nineteen, married and
discharged from the ATS, was found in a bed in a room
occupied by ten men in a US camp in the Forest. She was sent
to prison for three months.

In another instance some women were described as 'a menace
to a US camp'. They had been found, covered with a US blanket,
lying in a quarry. On another occasion a sergeant found the same
women in a hut near the camp at midnight. He told them to leave
but they were back within an hour and still there next day. The
Lydney magistrates sent them to prison for six months.

Some women were seen with coloured soldiers – which infuriated white troops. The British authorities had issued a directive: 'White women should not associate with coloured men. They should not walk out, dance or drink with them.'

Two sisters in a riverside parish did not mind if men were white or coloured, American or any other nationality. They did not walk out with them, neither did they dance, but rumour had it they did a brisk business down by the riverside and that the lane leading to their cottage was congested with jeeps. It was even said that the vicar stood at the end of the lane vainly trying to turn the men away.

In August 1942 *Advice to Americans About British Ways* was published. But the Foresters could have done with some advice about American ways too. They were shocked at the racial prejudice and the colour bar so rigorously enforced by white Americans. The British Government was also infected with racial prejudice. The Cabinet wanted the United States to 'reduce as soon as possible the number of coloured troops sent to Britain'. The Chiefs of Staff asked for the maximum number of white units; and Anthony Eden told the US Ambassador that 'our climate is badly suited to Negroes'.

On the other hand, Mrs Roosevelt, the American President's wife, was a champion of coloured Americans. She noticed that 'young southerners here are very indignant to find that the Negro soldiers were not looked upon with terror' by British girls.

Coloured US troops were stationed at Lydbrook and after he had left Lydbrook, a black sergeant wrote to the *Forest Newspapers* to say he had met with the 'most hospitality and geniality at Lydbrook'. He had been surprised at the 'complete non-existence of racial discrimination in Lydbrook', and he was amazed at

the high pedestal our Negro soldiers were put upon. The charming, intelligent English girls appeared as if it were an honour to be escorted to the dance by an American Negro soldier or a privilege to have them to tea on a Sunday afternoon. . . .

CHAPTER SEVENTEEN

PRISONERS OF WAR

It must have been 1942 when Italian prisoners of war arrived at the Wynals Hill Camp at Broadwell, which had recently been vacated by a motley collection of non-combatant soldiers of several different nationalities, most of whom had escaped from the Nazis. There were so many Italians coming to the camp that it soon had to be enlarged to contain them all.

The Italians were sent to work in the woods, acting as labourers for the Royal Engineers, or in the sawmills. The Italians were often blamed for cutting down the trees, and comments to that effect were often heard: 'It was the Italians who came and cut down our oaks' – Cinderford; 'It was the Italians who came and cut down our Chestnuts in 1943. We were told not to talk to them' – Popes Hill. But the Italians were not responsible for felling the oaks or the chestnuts and most people ignored the order not to speak to them.

The Italian prisoners were also sent to work on farms: 'We were glad to go, it gave us something to do instead of being shut up in the Camp.' Farmers gave them food and cigarettes although they were officially forbidden to do so. Eventually the Italians were giving cigarettes to the Foresters – they seemed to have a ready supply which they got from the Americans. Almost everybody liked the Italians; it would have been difficult not to like them.

Occasionally people got into trouble with the authorities because they were friendly with the Italian prisoners of war. One woman was sent to prison for a month because she dispatched written messages and cigarettes to an Italian whom she had met before the war and who became a prisoner in the Forest. It was also said that her action was 'likely to prejudice the discipline of a prisoner-of-war'. Another Forest woman was fined £1 for giving tea in her home to two prisoners of war.

Later on during the war, some former Italian prisoners declared themselves willing to assist the Allies. They were called 'co-operators'. At Lydney (there was a prison camp at Naas Lane), there were complaints about these co-operators. It was said that women were afraid to go into Bathurst Park because of being accosted by these men.

A letter dated October 1944 was sent to publicans in the Forest:

> It is reported that in some areas the Police have received instructions to see that Italian prisoners of war, many of whom are unaccompanied by guards, are *NOT* served with excisable liquors in licensed hours. You are therefore advised not to serve any of these prisoners of war or aliens under control.

One year my father had ten Italian prisoners of war to help with the sugar-beet harvest. They arrived every morning by lorry, and they did not have a guard with them. Nine went out to the field to pull, top or load sugar-beet into dung carts. (The sugar-beet was taken and put into clamps by the roadside, there to wait until a permit was granted when it could be taken and loaded into railway wagons.) The tenth Italian was their cook. The first thing he did was to search the orchards, fields and hedgerows for anything edible to put in his pot. It was late in the year, so there were only sour cider apples left in the orchards – unpeeled they went in the pot, peeled they were eaten raw. However, the orchard did yield bracket fungi which grew on the trunks of the trees. These and other strange fungi went into the pot. We told them they would all be poisoned, they smiled and said, 'OK, OK', and put them in the pot – and returned hale and hearty and smiling on the morrow. The cook often got very wet walking in the kale gathering the tops, again for the pot. Hardly any wood was safe when he started collecting fuel for the fire. They also brought food with them. One day it was bacon, which despite my father's entreaties they insisted on eating uncooked.

The other nine prisoners in their brown uniforms, with large patches of a different colour on the back of the coats and on the

The Marconi Monument, constructed by Italian prisoners of war at Coleford.

trousers, were out in the mud, the fog, and the cold misery of the sugar-beet field. None of us liked the sugar-beet harvest, but the Italians talked and laughed as they worked and occasionally burst into song. On wet days they crowded into a shed and sang and sang – opera had come to the farms of the Forest. They brought us baskets and rings they had made at the camp. Technically they were enemies, but really they were our friends.

The prisoners at Broadwell were keen footballers and played a number of Forest teams. Broadwell let the Italians use its football ground on Sundays. To the surprise of the local people the Italians had music at their matches, conveyed across the pitch by means of a tannoy.

The Italians decorated their own chapel in one of the huts and created a monument to Marconi. It was constructed out of whatever they could get – and this included stone and cement. It looked like marble, but was really cement painted white and flags of different nations were painted on its walls. The Italians were very

Guiseppe D'Ambrogio, Italian prisoner of war. He later worked on farms at Westbury.

Willi Zeighenheist, a German prisoner of war at Coleford in 1944 who later worked on a farm at Mitcheldean.

The interior of a Nissen hut at Coleford, converted into a chapel by the Italian prisoners. Most of the work was carried out by Faly Palmizi.

proud of it and everyone who saw it was impressed by it. It is gone now, but local people say it was disgraceful that it was demolished.

The German prisoners of war – 'those sad and sullen men' – came during the latter years of the war. There were guarded reports in the press about them. In 1944 the *Mercury* said: 'We hear that there are German prisoners of war in a camp not far from the banks of the Severn where the river runs through the Forest of Dean.' English people working alongside the prisoners had been ordered not to talk to them.

We had a few of these Germans to work on the farm and we did talk to them – as well as we could. Most of them, individually, were likeable men once they had 'thawed-out'. One of them – Big Willi we called him – was a farmer, an excellent worker, and showed us photographs of his wife and small children and talked wistfully of his small farm.

In March 1945 US troops, mounted police and officers on foot, hounds and Home Guard were searching the Forest of Dean for four German prisoners of war who were among seventy who had escaped from the Bridgend Camp on a Saturday. It was thought that a car found at Two Bridges had been used by the prisoners. Regular and Special Police, and American soldiers armed with tommy-guns searched the Forest, having first thrown a cordon round the wood at Two Bridges and not found the men in there. A squad of Specials on motor bikes came from Cheltenham and there was a constant patrol of police in cars.

Home Guards kept a watch on some roads. American soldiers held up vehicles and examined identity cards. A small Special at Newnham held up two boys riding bicycles from Littledean to Newnham and was prepared to arrest them on suspicion as they could not produce identity cards. That was on Sunday evening. On Monday evening the prisoners were sighted on Ruardean Hill. US troops and police searched until midnight on Wednesday. The fugitives had still not been recaptured. Eventually, however, the prisoners were apprehended.

CHAPTER EIGHTEEN

POLITICS

The Forest, like everywhere else, was bombarded with propaganda, orders, exhortations and advice; on hoardings, in newspapers, on leaflets, on the wireless and in films. The Ministry of Information (an odd name for an organization which suppressed as well as dispensed information) sent a travelling cinema round from time to time.

On 8 September 1939 the Chief Whips of the three main political parties signed an electoral truce, normal party politics were suspended and from May 1940 to May 1945 the three main parties of the British Government worked in coalition.

The Communist Party did a few about-turns. Before the war it had been a vigorous opponent of Fascism, and initially it supported the war against Germany. Then it opposed the war because it claimed it was an imperialist war. Its Party Secretary, Harry Pollitt, resigned because he disagreed with this opposition to the war against Fascism. When Russia entered the war the Party did another about-turn and vigorously supported the war against Germany. Harry Pollitt returned as Party Secretary and the Party observed the electoral truce. Within a year after the Battle of Leningrad and the Battle of Stalingrad the membership of the national Communist Party had trebled.

This popularity was reflected in the Forest. Perhaps the best indication of this is (in the absence of detailed figures etc.) the establishment of separate branches at Bream, Pillowell, Whitecroft and Yorkley. There was a branch at Cinderford (and probably other places) and a 'People's Bookshop' in Market Street. The popularity of the Communist Party was largely due to the sacrifices made by the Soviet people and a fervent identification with their cause. Another influence was the Forest

Miners' Unions' merger with the South Wales Miners' Federation; its leader, Arthur Horner, was a 'Communist firebrand' (who, incidentally, refused to support most wartime strikes). As the leader in the *Forest Newspapers* on 11 December 1942 said:

> The Communists, growing steadily in their numbers in this area, are now making their presence felt more strongly than any other political Party in the Forest.

Harry Pollitt came to the Forest on Saturday 18 October 1941 for a speaking engagement at the Bell Hotel, Ruardean. On Sunday morning he spoke again at the Memorial Hall, Broadwell, and in the evening at the Palace Cinema, Cinderford. He demanded greater output of war materials and the opening of the Second Front.

M.P. Price called the demand for a Second Front 'foolishness' and condemned 'the Forest agitators'. 'I have long since given up trying to find anything logical in the Communist policy,' he said.

In the autumn of 1941 the Forest of Dean Local Information Committee (in effect the Ministry of Information) organized 'War Commentary Meetings'. Mr M.P. Price spoke on Russia at Lydney, Cinderford and Coleford; Mr S.C. Jones spoke on the Far East at Lydney, Coleford and Cinderford; Miss Picton Turbeville spoke on Turkey at Newnham, Yorkley and Berry Hill; and the last of these meetings was the lecture given by Mr C.M. MacInnes on British–American Relations, at Yorkley, Newnham and Coleford.

In February 1942 Harry Pollitt returned to the Forest to speak at meetings at Bream, Yorkley and Drybrook. At the Palace, Cinderford, Arthur Horner spoke during a meeting at which the war situation, production, the Second Front, and the Beveridge Report was discussed. (The Beveridge Report proposed to abolish poverty by introducing a comprehensive programme of social security; Winston Churchill attempted to get the Report shelved.)

The Communist Party attempted affiliation with the Labour Party and an article by the Rt Hon. Arthur Greenwood MP

THE LABOUR PARTY

FIRST VISIT OF

MR. HAROLD LASKI

TO THE FOREST OF DEAN.

In these days when principles vital to the life of Democracy and Freedom are under discussion, it is more necessary than ever to be well informed. Your opportunity for extended information when Mr. Harold Laski, the well known writer, lecturer, Professor of Economics London University and Member of the National Executive Committee of the Labour Party, together with

MR. M. PHILIPS PRICE, M.P.

SPEAKS AS FOLLOWS : —

SAT., May 1st —WHITECROFT Memorial Hall	7 p.m
SUN., „ 2nd —COLEFORD Town Hall	2.45 „
„ „ „ —CINDERFORD Palace Picture House	7.30 „

Do not miss this visit of Mr. Laski.

COLLECTION.   10324

Mr Harold Laski visited the Forest in 1943.

saying why affiliation would be rejected by the Labour Party was published in the *Forest Newspapers*.

Labour held May Day meetings in 1943 on the Saturday and Sunday at Whitecroft, Coleford and Cinderford. Harold Laski was the speaker (this was his first visit to the Forest). The South Wales Miners' Federation held a May Day meeting in the clubroom at the Bell Hotel, Ruardean, where William Rust, editor of the *Daily Worker*, spoke.

In September 1943, 2,679 people in the Forest signed a petition organized by the Communist Party in support of the following: 5s. a day for every service man (in Forces), £2 for his wife, and 10s. per week for every dependent child. The Forest of Dean Area No. 9, Executive Committee of South Wales Miners' Federation, Cinderford Co-op Womens' Guild and Eastern United Miners' Lodge passed resolutions urging the adoption of the principle. A delegation of four wives of men in the Armed Forces presented the petition to M.P. Price MP at the Houses of Parliament.

Mr Price said he would not commit himself to the demands of the petition but would assist in every way to improve conditions for the serving man. (This seemed somewhat contradictory as one way to improve conditions would have been for Mr Price to commit himself to the demands of the petition.)

Towards the end of 1943, Oswald Mosley, the leader of the British Fascist Party was released after being interned. The Forest Miners' Executive protested against his release – 'Return No. 1 Fascist to his cage' – and protest meetings were held at Bream, Drybrook and Yorkley. In December the Communists had a meeting in Cinderford Town Hall. The Revd Dr Bryn Thomas was the principal speaker. (Bryn Thomas was the vicar at Kemble – 'The Bishop says I'm a good parson, but he doesn't like my politics'.) Admission was 6d. to the meeting, which was enlivened with musical items – the *Mercury* thought the Cinderford Communist Party should be called 'The Society for the Propagation of Brighter Political Meetings'.

Five May Day demonstrations, organized by the South Wales Miners' Federation (Area No. 9), were held in 1944. Tom Wintringham, the Vice-President of the Commonwealth Party, spoke at two of these meetings. Mr Wintringham was an original and forceful military theorist who had fought in the First World War and the Spanish Civil War; during the latter he had commanded the British Battalion of the International Brigade. He was the Military Correspondent of a national daily newspaper and a regular contributor to *Picture Post*. He had founded the Osterly Park Training School where he taught the elements of guerilla warfare to the Home Guard.

In March 1945 a Co-operative Party was formed at Cinderford. That same month at a meeting of the Westbury

Branch of the National Farmers' Union, Sir Lance Crawley-Boevey, the Chairman, said that if M.P. Price was nominated as a candidate at the next general election, 'as an agriculturalist he was worthy of their support'. But the miners were not prepared to give him their support.

At a May Day meeting that year, the miners' agent, John Williams, said that the Miners' Executive had asked him to announce that it was the miners' intention to exercise their rights to nominate a candidate for the next parliamentary election through the Forest of Dean Divisional Labour Party. The miners wanted a candidate who was a worker, a trade unionist, and a man who could devote the whole of his time to the parliamentary work of the constituency.

Mr Williams said:

Nationalization of the mines would be an important issue at the next election. The wages of the miners from 1926 to 1939 were disgracefully low, they were among the lowest paid workers in the country, notwithstanding the fact that the work is notoriously dangerous and arduous. For years the average wage in this district was 8/3d a shift.

Mr G.T.D. Jenkins, a member of the Forest of Dean Miners' Executive, said the Forest coalfield was becoming exhausted and this was a fact that was not generally appreciated when criticism was levelled at the miners about their output.

At a subsequent Labour Party meeting, Mr S.T. Skelton of Longhope (and a member of Westbury NFU) moved that M.P. Price be invited to become the Labour candidate again. John Williams, however, opposed the motion. A vote was taken: there were sixty-six votes for Price and thirty-one against. At a further meeting held at Parkend, all the delegates, about one hundred, voted unanimously in favour of M.P. Price, who was then adopted as the Labour candidate.

The Communists held a meeting at Whitecroft (the Pillowell band paraded to the meeting and played during the proceedings). All-out support for the Forest Labour candidate was urged by George Thomas, member of the District Committee of the

FOR VICTORY & A NEW LIFE

THE COMMUNIST POLICY EXPLAINED
BY

GEORGE THOMAS
Organisation Department, South Wales.

REG EVANS
Organiser Forest of Dean Sub-District.

WELFARE HALL, WHITECROFT
SUNDAY, FEB. 27th, at 7.30 p.m.

Organised by the Whitecroft Branch, Communist Party.

Mr George Thomas spoke on behalf of the Communist Party, which was popular in the Forest during the war.

Communist Party. Members heeded Mr Thomas's advice and also gave their support to the Labour candidate. Following this, it was generally thought that M.P. Price would be unopposed – as neither the Conservatives nor the Liberals had declared their intentions.

Then on 4 June, in the *Citizen,* it was reported that at a meeting

of representatives from the Constituency, this meeting of supporters of the National Government, having considered the matter, has decided that the seat shall be contested in the National interests.

These nameless supporters of the National Government then had to find a candidate. Mr John Watts, the well-known Lydney businessman, declined to stand in opposition to M.P. Price. Mr Watts made it quite clear that had he stood it would be clearly as an Independent – he would not fight the election on behalf of any political party.

A week or so later a candidate was produced to oppose M.P. Price. He was Sgt Major John Brown of the Royal Armoured Corps. He had once been a pit-head worker at a Tyneside Colliery, had spent two years on the dole, gained a Trade Union Scholarship to Oxford, and fought unsuccessfully as a Labour candidate in 1935.

At a meeting at Speech House, Sgt Major Brown was introduced by Sir Lance Crawley-Boevey and his adoption was formally moved by Mr John Watts who emphasized that Mr Brown was not a Conservative candidate but an Independent supporting Mr Churchill (the Conservative leader).

Mr Brown's slogan was 'Tell the truth and leave it to the people'. In a letter published in the *Mercury*, Mr Stigwood of Cinderford appeared to be doubtful of Mr Brown's slogan. He asked if Mr Brown were truly independent or if he and his agent were backed by a political party as he had never known an agent to be appointed before a political candidate except on a party basis.

Mr Stigwood then wrote a second letter asking another question.

On Saturday last, Mr Brown's first Cinderford meeting took place and the principal speaker was Col Mitchell, Conservative MP for Brentford and Vice-Chairman of the Conservative Party, but this was not mentioned at the meeting – why?

As far as I know, Mr Stigwood did not receive any answers to his questions.

On the day Mr Stigwood's letter was published, Mr Brown spoke at Lydney Town Hall:

We shall leave it to other people to make the windy promises and wave their blood-red banners. Germany swallowed wholesale the promises of the National Socialist Party and you can see now where it has ended.

M.P. Price polled 19,721 votes. J. Brown polled 10,529 votes.

POSTSCRIPT

When the war was over the GIs went home, and by and by the Forest girls they had married went to America too. The Americans left the poison gas behind and it was several years before it was moved. Traces of the American 'invasion' remain. At Wimbury Slade, near Mile End, US rifle butts can still be seen, and American ammunition (British as well) has been found there.

From the Dilke Hospital to Speech House, along Spruce Drive, and through Cannop, rifle rounds, carbines, machine gun rounds, grenades and mortar shells have been found. A shell with fins was found in March 1995. Furniture from the US camp at Pingry Lane, Coleford, was dumped down an old mine shaft near Sling.

The British soldiers went away too and the hardwoods that they felled have been replaced by conifers, which look like serried ranks of green soldiers. Not all the soldiers went away, some married local girls and came back to the Forest. Forest men who returned often found nowhere to live with their families.

Three ex-Service men and their families moved into the ex-US army camp at Naas Farm, Lydney, in August 1946. They were the first 'squatters' to settle here after the war. (The Forest had squatters in the past but now, all over the country, people desperate for accommodation were moving into empty buildings.)

The ex-US camp was bought by Lydney Industrial Estate Ltd, to house key-workers coming to the area for the development of new industries. The controller of this estate met the squatters and told them they were on private property. 'For every key-worker who comes to live on this estate, thirty semi-skilled Forest of Dean people will be employed,' he said. 'If you remain here, you will prejudice industrial development.' The squatters left – two of the families moved into the Nissen hut near Allastone Mesne, which the Home Guard had used as a store. A *Mercury* reporter wrote:

> I admire these families for their determination, for making the best of a bad job – a bad job because here, amongst many others in England today, were two ex-Servicemen who deserved something better.

People, including an ex-Serviceman who had survived the Arnhem fiasco, moved into ex-army huts on the Cinderford Recreational Ground. The squatters selected a hut and wrote their surnames on the door. All day on Saturday 17 August 1946 families dragged furniture in to the huts. Here they stayed, some families for several years. It was better than nothing and better than overcrowded apartments, but it was not much of a reward for soldiers returning from the war.

ACKNOWLEDGEMENTS

I am grateful to the following for various kinds of help:

E. Ball, J. Ball, F. Beard, C. Betterton, J. Billings, H. Bishop, C. Boughton, M. Burns, I. Cadogan, R. Chuter, N. Cook, R. Cooper, G. D'Ambrogio, C. Dix, W. Dobbins, A. Eagles, P. Eley, H. Geddes, R. & N. Gould, J. Hale, L. Hale, M. Harris, S. Harris, B. Hobman, K. Holder, H. Hopkins, J. Joseph, G. Kettle, D. King, K. Lander, R. Lewis, B. Littleton, J. Marrot, V. Martin, R. Minchin, D. Morris, R. Moseley, E. Olivey, J. Pritchard, M. Reynolds, J. Roberts, I. Ryder, N. Sinfield, B. Sysum, J. Tobin, L. Tuffley, E. Warren, M. Watts, F. Wherrett, A. White, R. Williams, W. Williams, J. Worgan, A. Wright.

I am also indebted to J. Bright for kindly allowing me to quote from the wartime issues of the three Forest newspapers and to W.H. Tandy for the extracts from his book *A Doctor in the Forest*.

Photograph credits: My thanks to L. Baber, C. Boughton, H. Boughton, M. Burns, N. Cook, G. D'Ambrogio, E. Davies, N. Gould, M. Haile, M. Harvey, A. Keyse, J. Littleton, R. Minchin, R. Moseley, E. Olivey, L. Tuffley, M. Watts, A. White, A. Wright.

I tender my thanks to all these people, without whom this book could not have been completed. For anyone who has been inadvertently omitted I offer my sincere apologies.